William John Townsend

Madagascar

It's Missionaries And Martyrs

William John Townsend

Madagascar
It's Missionaries And Martyrs

ISBN/EAN: 9783742810649

Manufactured in Europe, USA, Canada, Australia, Japa

Cover: Foto ©Lupo / pixelio.de

Manufactured and distributed by brebook publishing software (www.brebook.com)

William John Townsend

Madagascar

MADAGASCAR

Its Missionaries and Martyrs

BY

WILLIAM JOHN TOWNSEND, D.D.

AUTHOR OF "THE GREAT SCHOOLMEN OF THE MIDDLE AGES;" "ROBERT MORRISON, THE PIONEER OF CHINESE MISSIONS," ETC.

NEW YORK AND CHICAGO.
Fleming H. Revell Company,
PUBLISHERS OF EVANGELICAL LITERATURE.

PREFACE.

THE marvellous story of Christianity in the Island of Madagascar is one that should be familiar to all who take an interest in the growing kingdom of the Lord Jesus. The young people of the Churches and Sunday-schools especially should read the story, that their enthusiasm in holy work may be quickened. It is with this object that these pages have been written. The facts here recorded have been gathered from many sources, but mainly from the "History of Madagascar," in 2 vols., compiled from original documents, by Rev. W. Ellis, a valuable repertory of information relating to the subject; "Three Visits to Madagascar," and "The Martyr Church," also by Rev. W. Ellis; "Madagascar and its People," by Mr. J. Sibree; and "Madagascar:

Its Missions and its Martyrs," by Rev. E. Prout. The excellent article on Madagascar in the invaluable "Encyclopædia of Missions," recently issued by Messrs. Funk & Wagnalls, with the reports and periodicals of various Missionary Societies, have also supplied many of the facts herein related. The writer earnestly hopes that this little book may contribute to the deepening interest in Missions, which is the most cheering characteristic of this century.

W. J. TOWNSEND.

CONTENTS.

CHAPTER I.
MADAGASCAR AND ITS PEOPLE .   PAGE 9

CHAPTER II.
INTRODUCTION OF CHRISTIANITY   24

CHAPTER III.
THE GOSPEL ROOTING ITSELF—GATHERING STORM   47

CHAPTER IV.
THE NOBLE ARMY OF MARTYRS   72

CHAPTER V.
THE FIRE OF SUCCESSIVE PERSECUTIONS . . 87

CONTENTS.

CHAPTER VI.

	PAGE
THE DAWN OF FREEDOM AND PROSPERITY	110

CHAPTER VII.

| A CHRISTIAN KINGDOM ESTABLISHED | 138 |

CHAPTER VIII.

| PROGRESS, PAST AND PRESENT | 155 |

MADAGASCAR:

ITS MISSIONARIES AND MARTYRS.

CHAPTER I.

MADAGASCAR AND ITS PEOPLE.

"The kingdom of heaven is compared, not to any great kernel or nut, but to a grain of mustard seed, which is one of the least of grains, but hath in it a property and spirit hastily to set up and spread."—*Lord Bacon.*

MADAGASCAR is the third largest island in the world. It lies in the Indian Ocean, about three hundred miles from the south-east coast of Africa, from which it is separated by the Mozambique Channel. It is 980 miles long, and in its broadest part, which is near the middle, is 350 miles across. Its area is nearly four times larger than that of England and Wales.

Its physical configuration is very varied. There is an elevated mountainous region, occupying a large portion of the interior, and this contains four ranges of mountains, stretching from north to south irregularly. The highest mountains, one of which rises 9000 feet above the level of the sea, are in Imerina. There are several peaks which rise from 5000 to 6000 feet, and present a grandly picturesque appearance. This hilly region is in every respect the finest part of the island. The climate here is delightful; beautiful plains and valleys, carefully cultivated and wonderfully fertile, stretch out in many directions, and in this district also the people are the most industrious and intelligent.

As might readily be supposed from the numerous hills and mountains, the island is watered by many streams and rivers, although, for want of sufficient depth, few of them can be used for purposes of navigation. On the eastern side a long chain of lagoons extends for nearly 300 miles, and small lakes exist here and there, the largest of which is twenty-five miles in length.

The island is of volcanic origin, and recent research has discovered a volcanic range extending over a great part of the mainland, and although no active volcano now exists, there is no doubt that in past times the country has been subject to violent eruptions. The geological formations consist of granite, gneiss, and basalt. The general aspect of the country is that of bare rolling moors, interspersed with stretches of bright red and brown clay lands. But immediately below the hilly region is a dense forest belt which extends almost entirely round the island, and contains many kinds of valuable timber. The climate in the low country stretching down to the coast is hot and damp, producing malaria and miasma of very fatal nature.

NATIVES POUNDING RICE.

The *flora* and *fauna* of Madagascar are most abundant. Hundreds of species have been found which are peculiar to it, and very many are of rare beauty. About 250 varieties of ferns have been discovered, and the list is far from complete. Orchids are innumerable and unrivalled for their beauty. The country is a happy hunting-ground both for botanists and entomologists, as plant life and insect life generally exist side by side in abundance and variety.

The smaller birds and animals abound in endless varieties, but there are none of the larger beasts of prey to be found. There are a few large birds of prey, but the numerous small birds are of beautiful plumage, and mostly peculiar to the island. Cattle, sheep, pigs, and poultry have been naturalised during the last two centuries, and are now as common as in England. Almost all kinds of food and fruit are produced which grow in China and India. Rice is the staple food of the people, and is very plentiful.

The people of Madagascar, called the Malagasy, are sprung from the Malays — Polynesian stock rather than African, although it is most likely the original inhabitants were from South Africa. It is supposed that the present race came to the island at different times and gradually overpowered or supplanted the first inhabitants. They are divided into numerous tribes, who all speak the same language, although, as in England, several dialects are found. There was no written character and consequently no books or manuscripts until Christian missionaries reduced the language to writing sixty years ago.

Whilst the people were not civilised until they had the arts and customs of civilised life introduced to them through Christianity, they have never been disgraced by the barbarism of many heathen islanders. They maintained a form of government of a feudal character. The land and the people were in the hands of the nobles, the rulers were moderate in the exercise of their authority, and the people were law-abiding in their civil life. There were several powerful tribes which occupied the chief part of the island, and which were sub-divided into numerous clans. These tribes, under the command of their own chieftains, sometimes waged war upon their neighbours, causing great loss of life, not only by the battles fought, but even more still by the starvation and fever which nearly always were consequent upon the strife.

The great blot upon the social life of the Malagasy was their system of slavery. A large portion of the population was enslaved, comprising chiefly bankrupt debtors and prisoners of war, and a considerable slave trade was kept up with the Arab dealers. The chief employment of the people was agriculture, but several handicrafts were practised, such as spinning, weaving, and working in metals. Their houses were built chiefly of hard red clay, with high pitched roofs, thatched with grass or rushes. After the introduction of Christianity a considerable import and export trade sprang up between them and European traders.

Although the people at the commencement of the present century were not sunken in the revolting immoralities which characterised some of the islanders of the Pacific, yet their morals were in many respects exceedingly low. Polygamy was generally practised and chastity unknown. Theft, trickery, and lying were almost universal, whilst masses of the people were incorrigibly lazy. Infanticide was frequent, and drunkenness prevalent in some parts of the island. Human life and suffering were reckoned of no account, and punishment by death in cruel forms was inflicted for trivial crimes.

It can scarcely be said that the Malagasy had any system of religion or belief. They believed in an Almighty Being who was the ruler of all things, and they had rude ideas concerning lesser deities who presided over certain localities or particular interests. But they had no forms of worship, no temples, scarcely any idols, no priesthood and no ceremonial. Their language contains some traces of an ancient belief in the leading truths of natural religion, but in later times the recognition of these had died out. Their idolatry took the form of Fetichism, and they believed in charms, as having the power to protect them from evil or to confer benefits upon them. They practised divination and witchcraft, and they had curious ordeals for the detection of crime. Great sacrifices of fowls and sheep were made at harvest time, and a tradition exists that on important occasions, human sacrifices were offered by the coast tribes. A large class of people existed as sorcerers, diviners, and tellers of unlucky days and signs, who lived upon the superstitious feelings of the people.

A very curious account is given of the state idols, by Mrs. Ellis, who saw them borne in the procession at the coronation of King Radama II. She says:—
" There were about thirteen in number, and were carried on tall, slender poles about ten feet high. There was in most of them little resemblance to any-

thing in heaven or in earth. Dirty pieces of silver chain; silver balls from the size of a marble to that of a hen's egg; pieces of coral or bone, or silver ornaments intended to represent shark's teeth, with narrow strips of scarlet cloth one or two feet long—such were the objects on which the security and prosperity of the nation were formerly supposed to depend."* A very interesting description of the destruction of the national idols in 1869 is given by one present on the occasion, who describes the chief idol as being "a piece of wood two or three inches long, and as large as the middle finger of a man's hand, wrapped in two thicknesses of scarlet silk about three feet long and three inches wide, the wood pointed at one end, and movable in the silk, with two silver chains, about three inches in length, at either end of the silk. It was placed in a small case made of a portion of a young tree hollowed out. There was no carving or ornamental work upon it. This idol was the guardian of the sovereign and of the kingdom; others, as that protecting against serpents, that preserving the rice crop from harm, etc., were still more rude than that already described."†

Persons suspected of witchcraft were subjected to the tangena, or poison ordeal. Political offenders were made to undergo the same test. The tangena nut was a powerful poison, but it acted only as a violent emetic if administered in minute doses. Innocence was supposed to be declared by the vomiting of three small pieces of fowl which had been swallowed whole. The suspected person first ate a quantity of rice, and then

---

* "Madagascar: its Social and Religious Progress," by Mrs. Ellis, 1863.

† "Encyclopædia of Missions," vol. ii. p. 7.

a portion of the tangena nut was scraped into the juice of a banana. A prayer was offered by the accuser to the spirit of the poison, containing the most terrible imprecations, but the strain of which was to the effect that, if the accused were guilty, the guilt might be revealed, but if innocent, the three pieces of fowl received might be rejected. If they were not, the culprit was beaten to death, and the body buried in a degrading manner, or left to be devoured by dogs. More than one-fourth of those who underwent the ordeal died from its effects, and of those who survived many experienced serious affliction for the remainder of their lives.

The capital of Madagascar is Antananarivo, the largest city in the island, and containing about 100,000 inhabitants. It has been entirely rebuilt since the introduction of Christianity, and is now a fine city, with royal palaces and government offices, four handsome churches built in memory of the Christian martyrs, whose history will be related in subsequent pages of this volume, with many other important edifices, such as the College, the schools, and hospitals of the London Missionary Societies. Next in importance to the capital is the city of Mojanga in the north-west, with 14,000 people. Tamatave is the principal port on the east coast, with a population of 6000. Some other towns are scattered over the island, with populations of 5000 downwards, and the whole number of the people is estimated at 5,000,000.

In the year 1702, a ship sailing from London to India was wrecked on the south-east coast of Madagascar near Port Dauphine. Many of the passengers and crew escaped with their lives, and dispersing over the mainland were heard of no more. A boy named Robert Drury, then fourteen years of age, after enduring great suffering, became a domestic slave in the households of various native masters, experiencing alternate kindness and cruelty at their hands.

He afterwards recorded, in a very simple and natural manner, much interesting information as to the character and habits of the islanders, and it is to him that the English owe their first knowledge of Madagascar and its inhabitants. He narrates that after he escaped from the wreck, the group of survivors with whom he was associated were taken before the chief of that part of the island and put to death in the most barbarous manner, he alone being preserved alive. He remained in slavery for several years, being employed in tending cattle, driving them to and from the water, slaughtering them, digging wild yams, and cultivating bees. Yearning for freedom, he seized an opportunity of making his escape, and fled to a seaport on the western coast. Here he was seized by a chieftain, and trained to fight in his service. After fifteen years' exile, he was ransomed by his parents, with whom he had been able to communicate through some visitors calling at the port, and to his unspeakable joy, he returned to his native land. Very much of the information we possess concerning the Malagasy is due to the interesting narrative of Robert Drury.

During the seventeenth and eighteenth centuries the most powerful tribe was the Sakalàva, which was divided into two great branches, the Northern and the Southern. The tribes of the Hovas and the Betsileos

ANTANANARIVO.

were heavily oppressed by the Sakalàva and regarded with supreme contempt. Indeed, they were reckoned as the lowest and most degraded of all the tribes upon the island. The district they inhabited was called Imerina, and in 1785 the chief of the Hovas succeeded in uniting the whole of the tribes of this district under his command. He then attached to himself several tribes or clans in the adjacent districts, and so became the leader of a formidable confederacy; he was strengthening his position, with a view to throwing off the dominion of the Sakalàvas, when he was attacked by a fatal sickness. He hastily summoned home his son Radama, then seventeen years of age, and who was under the care of Arab teachers, and on the father's decease, this boy was proclaimed chief or king in his stead.

Radama had early given proof of much shrewdness and tenderness of disposition. When he was a little child his father and mother quarrelled, with the result that his mother was divorced, and sent home to her father. One day, when his father was absent, the boy got a chicken and tied it to the leg of a chair. When his father returned he asked who had done this, and was told it was Radama. The child was called, and asked what he meant by his action. He answered, " It was a little chicken crying for its mother." The father took the hint, sent for his wife, and reinstated her in her position.

The early life of Radama was remarkable for its temperance and purity. The father thought this the evidence of a feeble mind, and actually offered bribes to those who could succeed in leading his son into vice. There were but too many base beguilers ready for the vile work, and they pursued it with such success that in a few years a healthy constitution was destroyed, and a life terminated, which might have been a blessing and an honour to the nation.

Radama was a man of extraordinary qualities. He was energetic, ambitious, shrewd, had a keen insight

TYPES OF MALAGASY.

into human nature, and he possessed the remarkable power of attaching men to himself, and bending them to his purposes. He imbibed from his father the desire to cast off the yoke of the Sakalàvas, and thus to become the king of the whole nation.

During his reign, from 1810 to 1828, he gained possession of two-thirds of the island. But he saw clearly that, if he were fully to realise his purpose, he must have an army supplied with fire-arms, and trained in European drill and tactics. During the war between England and France, the neighbouring islands of Mauritius and Bourbon came into the possession of the English, and this acquisition included the surrender of some French dependencies in Madagascar, which had been established many years before. The new governor of the Mauritius, Sir Robert Farquhar, was earnestly desirous of abolishing the slave trade in the Indian Ocean, of which Madagascar was the chief seat. Radama entered into a treaty with him to stop the export of slaves on condition that he received in compensation a supply of British arms, ammunition, and uniforms, as well as training for his soldiers. He sent a number of youths to be trained in England and in Mauritius, and an English agent, Mr. Hastie, was despatched to reside at Antananarivo, who cordially co-operated with the king in promoting the material interests of the country.

Radama during his reign succeeded in making himself master of the whole island with the exception of two districts in the south. Thus political unity was accomplished as a preparation through Providence for the propagation of Christianity. The king was at once a skilful soldier and a wise statesman. He had become convinced of the superiority of European civilisation, and earnestly laboured to introduce many forms of it into his kingdom. If in his private life he had kept free from vice, he might have lived to have matured the reforms he introduced, but indulgence in drink and licentiousness of living cut him down before he had reached his prime.

CHAPTER II.

INTRODUCTION OF CHRISTIANITY.

"There never was found in any age of the world, either philosopher, or sect, or law, or discipline which did so highly exalt the public good as the Christian faith."—*Lord Bacon.*

MADAGASCAR was discovered by the Portuguese in 1506. They established a colony there, and introduced some Romish priests, who sought to propagate their religion in the eastern provinces. The French broke up the Portuguese settlement, and the Romish mission was abandoned. But about the middle of the seventeenth century another attempt was made to convert the people to the Roman Catholic faith. A bishop, with a company of priests and other helpers, sought to mission the tribes along the east coast, but without much success. After some time the effort came to a disastrous end. The leader of the priests was not content to allow the Gospel to win its way legitimately with the people, but sought to force the process of conversion by commanding them to abandon their evil practices, and threatening them with the vengeance

INTRODUCTION OF CHRISTIANITY. 25

of the French if they refused. The result was that the priest and his followers were ruthlessly put to death. A decimating slaughter by the French followed this impolitic act, and thus cruelty and persecution became associated in the minds of the natives with the very name of Christianity. This feeling lingered even to the present century, and made the introduction of the Gospel in the island somewhat more difficult than otherwise would have been the case.

At the close of the last century the London Missionary Society was engaged in wistfully scanning every part of the heathen world to discover where it might best disseminate a knowledge of Christ and disperse the gloom of idolatry and barbarism. It had its attention early aroused to the claims and needs of Madagascar, and in 1796 it began to gather information as to the island, its climate, and its inhabitants.

In 1798, when Dr. Vanderkemp sailed for South Africa, he received instructions to use any practicable means to facilitate the commencement of a mission among the Malagasy, and in 1799 he wrote to the Committee stating that as the result of his inquiries he was prepared to strongly recommend the immediate sending out of three or four agents. Nothing was done in the matter for several years until Dr. Vanderkemp, being so impressed with the importance of the work, decided in spite of his advanced years and the perils of the undertaking to go there himself. While he was making preparations for this purpose, his noble career was terminated by death.

Not till 1817 were definite steps taken towards the desired end. Then the Committee appointed the Revs. S. Bevan and D. Jones to proceed to Madagascar and attempt missionary work. They had both been students under Rev. M. Philips of Newodalwyd, and removed from thence to complete their missionary training under Rev. Dr. Bogue at Gosport. They were ordained for the work, at Menaddlwyd, Cardiganshire, in August, 1817, and they sailed for Mauritius in February, 1818, arriving there in July. Leaving their wives and infant children at Mauritius, the two missionaries sailed for Madagascar and reached Tamatave on the 18th of August. They had been much discouraged by the many unfavourable representations of the country they had received from all quarters, but bravely they resolved to risk the attempt and enter it in the name of Jesus.

On landing they were introduced to Jean René, the chief of Tamatave, and Mr. Bragg an English trader who was settled there. René was not sanguine as to their object, but undertook to use his influence on their behalf. He advised them to write to King Radama, asking permission to commence work in his neighbourhood, but explained that just then the king was greatly incensed against the English because of a violation of the treaty he had entered into with them. Therefore some opposition and even danger might be anticipated in his province.

The missionaries decided that, as a first step, they would commence their operations in Tamatave. Mr. Bragg invited them to his extensive residence, about a mile out of the city, and after reconnoitring a few days, they began to take steps towards the establishment of a mission. They visited Fisatra, the chief of a neighbouring village called Hivondrona, who gave them a cordial welcome, and promised to place his son under their tuition. This example was soon followed by many of the leading people in the neighbourhood. Mr. Bragg undertook to erect a mission house, and set about the work with such earnestness, that by the 8th of September it was finished, and a school opened in it with six children. This number afterwards increased, and the missionaries were greatly pleased with the intelligence and docility of their pupils, as were the parents with the course of instruction, but especially with the singing.

Messrs. Bevan and Jones having thus as they hoped auspiciously opened their work, returned to Mauritius, leaving their school in the care of Mr. Bragg, who, strange to say, dismissed the pupils immediately the missionaries had left. On arriving at Mauritius, they found their wives enduring much reproach on account of the work their husbands had undertaken. Mr. Jones and his family therefore hastened to leave for Madagascar, but Mr. Bevan was detained for some time at St. Louis, the chief town of Mauritius, by the illness of his wife. When Mr. and Mrs. Jones reached Tamatave on the 19th of October, they were saluted by cries of "Welcome, welcome." They were gratified to find, that notwithstanding the closing of the school, the work was in progress, for the children who had attended it were engaged in imparting their knowledge to others, and were anxiously awaiting the arrival of the missionaries that they might begin again.

Prince, or Chief René kindly granted a piece of ground for the building of a school-house, and a commencement of it was made. But the season was very unhealthy, heavy rains drenched the ground, the house built by Mr. Bragg was damp, and the result was that the whole missionary household were laid low with the terrible Malagasy fever. On the 13th of December, the infant daughter of Mr. Jones died; on the 29th his wife also was taken from him, and he was so ill that he was not expected to survive. Early in January, Mr. Bevan with his wife and infant arrived at Tamatave. On landing he was told abruptly of the deaths of Mrs. Jones and her infant. The tidings greatly affected him, and he stood before the house where Mr. Jones lay apparently dying and wept bitterly.

From that moment he was possessed with a presentiment that he should fall a victim to the devouring pestilence. Before the month of January closed he and his little child were filling one grave, and in the following month his pious, sorrowing wife went to join them in their heavenly home. Before Mr. Bevan passed away he said to Mr. Jones, "I shall certainly die, but you will recover and proceed with your work, and ultimately succeed in the Mission." The spirit of prophecy was upon him in the utterance of these words, as none could have been more happily fulfilled.

Mr. Jones was now the only member of the Mission party remaining, and the circumstances in which he was left were sufficiently mournful. But they were rendered more aggravating by the singular conduct of Mr. Bragg. He turned against Mr. Jones and the Mission without any ostensible reason, and heaped upon him every form of insult and ridicule. As a result of his conduct, the property of the Mission was stolen, and parties came into the house scoffing at the calamities which had befallen the missionary, and eating up his provisions. The helpless invalid bore up bravely under these trials, and when his strength was sufficiently recruited he crawled to Tamatave, where he begged from a friendly native a shelter from the persecution of Mr. Bragg. But his retreat was discovered, and Mr. Bragg followed him to it, had him conveyed back to his house by force, and systematically illtreated him, until frequent relapses of fever and prolonged unkindness so reduced his strength as to render recovery in Madagascar impossible. Therefore, he sailed for Mauritius on the 3rd of July, receiving much kindness from the chief Fisatra, and many good wishes from friendly natives.

Mr. Jones stayed in Mauritius fourteen months. He had careful medical attendance, and received great help from an English resident, who afforded him assistance in studying the Malagasy language. Mr. Jones meantime repaid the kindness by collecting seventy children on the gentleman's estate and teaching them.

During his absence, events were moving swiftly in Madagascar. A Frenchman landed at Tamatave, and making his way to the capital, presented handsome gifts to Radama, urging him to allow the French to open out their former trade. Sir Robert Farquhar was absent from Mauritius at the time, having gone on a visit to England, and a weak and foolish man, General Hall, was invested with authority in his absence. This man sent back to Radama the youths who had come to Mauritius to be trained and educated, thereby giving deep offence to Radama, and leading him to permit the recommencement of the slave trade which Sir Robert had striven so earnestly to suppress.

When Sir Robert returned to his post in July, 1820, he took early steps to renew the treaty with Radama for the complete suppression of the slave trade and of slavery. The king was vigorously pursuing his policy of conquest, and had forced several powerful tribes, among which were the Sakalàvas, into submission, when Mr. Jones, accompanied by Mr. James Hastie, the English envoy appointed by Sir Robert Farquhar to negotiate the treaty, arrived at the port of Tamatave. They quickly set out for Antananarivo, and arrived there early in October. Mr. Hastie was received by Radama with great state and pomp, and on Mr. Jones being introduced he was greeted with a cordial welcome. In a few days a new treaty was prepared and concluded between the king and the English Government for the suppression of the shameful slave traffic, and on its ratification the English flag was hoisted on the royal palace, and a royal salute fired. Radama also assured Mr. Jones that he might remain in the capital, and that any other missionaries who came to help him would receive protection. Mr. Hastie greatly rejoiced in the auspicious consummation of his mission. He said in his despatch announcing the news: " I declare the first peal of Radama's cannon announcing the amity sealed rejoiced my heart more than the gift of thousands would have done."

On the 8th of December, 1820, Mr. Jones commenced his work by opening a school in the capital. He began with three pupils but next day more were added, and daily he had fresh recruits. Then arrangements were made to build a residence for the missionary, and the king himself laid the foundation of it and sprinkled it with sacred water—a rite of long standing in the

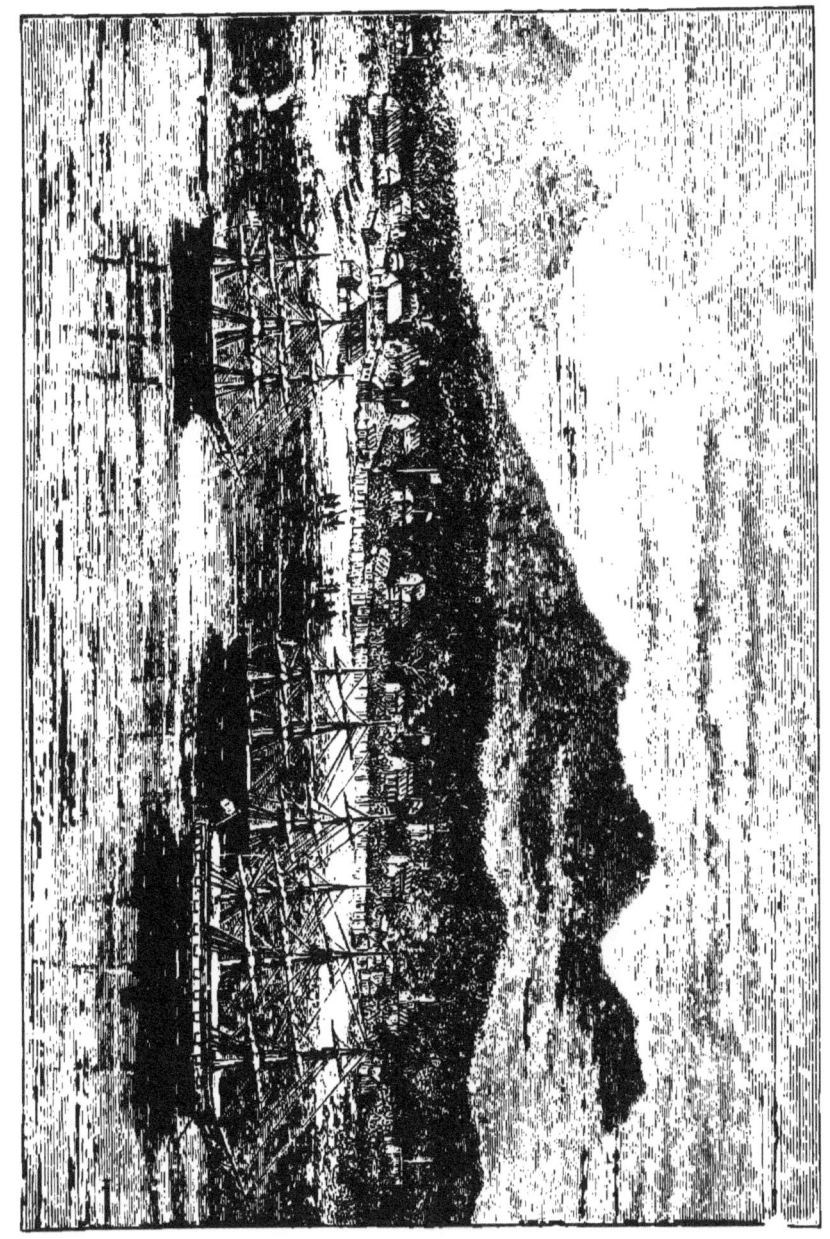

TAMATAVE.

INTRODUCTION OF CHRISTIANITY. 33

country. This office Radama fulfilled that he might offer his token of respect for the work of the missionary and rebuke any prejudice the people might have concerning it.

In the middle of May, 1821, Rev. David Griffiths who had been sent out by the London Missionary Society to assist in the work, arrived at Tamatave, accompanied by a small band of European artisans. They at once set out for Antananarivo escorted by Mr. Hastie, and were cheered by several messages of welcome from the king on their journey. On their arrival they were received by him with every token of respect. Mr. Griffiths took up his abode in the mission-house with Mr. Jones. There were twenty-two pupils in the school, all selected from the families of the king and his nobility. Several had learned to read the Bible and had made satisfactory progress in several branches of knowledge. Radama was delighted with their singing and used often to come into the school to listen to them. He frequently announced the hymn to be sung. He gave orders that this should be called " The Royal School."

After due consideration it was resolved that Mr. Griffiths should take charge of the school while Mr. Jones paid a visit to the Isle of France for the benefit of his health, and that he should afterwards commence another school for the children of the people. It was agreed with Radama, who carefully discussed every point, that on the arrival of Mrs. Griffiths, who was expected soon, the girls should be instructed in needlework and other useful household attainments. In August, Mr. Griffith went to Tamatave to meet his wife and escort her to the capital. The king showed him abounding kindness in preparing for the journey, one of Radama's sisters sent her servants to carry his provisions, and a few of the pupils went with him for some miles of the way.

When Mr. Griffith started, the king had gone from the capital on a warlike expedition, but the missionary left a letter for him expressing his fervent gratitude for the friendly attentions he had rendered, and begging him to make further provision for the Mission in the erection of schools and houses. To this letter Radama sent a gracious reply promising all that was desired.

On the 10th of October the missionary party, consisting of Mr. Jones and his recently married wife, Mr. and Mrs. Griffith and their infant child, Mr. Barnsley, assistant agent, and another, arrived at Antananarivo. Mr. Hastie came to meet them, bearing a letter of welcome from the king. Twelve of the royal servants also met them carrying refreshments. Mr. Hastie took the infant and carried it, saying, "I shall take the first white child into the capital of Madagascar." The party proceeded to the palace amidst crowds of spectators and shouts of welcome. As they entered the courtyard, the king, his mother, and sister, cordially received them.

Next day the king presented a site for a new mission-house. The people at once set to work to level the ground and prepare for building. Then Mr. Griffiths commenced his school. He chose eleven boys and four girls from the chief families in the city. These were all clothed lightly as Europeans, and their education proceeded apace.

Mr. Jones, although suffering from a relapse of fever,

reopened his school in the presence of Radama, who sat during the examination of the children in all the subjects which they had been taught, and then expressed himself as being delighted with the progress they had made. The missionaries were also greatly cheered by the kindness of Sir R. Farquhar who arranged that the whole expense of the missionaries' journey from Mauritius to the capital should be borne by the English Government and who also authorised Mr. Jones to draw thirty dollars per month for the support of the schools which had been opened.

In accordance with an ancient custom in the island, of presenting the king with the first-fruits of the field, Mrs. Griffith, on the 21st of December, 1821, presented Radama with the first piece of needlework which her pupils had completed. He expressed great gratification with it and in return gave each of the girls a piece of money.

Mr. Hastie being about to return to Mauritius, Radama arranged for twenty carefully selected youths to proceed for education, ten to Mauritius, and ten to England. Prince Ratefy, brother-in-law to the king, was going to England as ambassador, and the youths intended for this country accompanied him. On their arrival, they were placed under the care of the London Missionary Society. Radama had also sent by Ratefy an earnest request that the Society would send out more missionaries, but especially more artisans and artificers to teach in Madagascar the useful arts of western civilisation. Accordingly the Rev. J. Jeffreys and his wife, with four skilled workmen, returned with the Prince when his mission in England was concluded.

On the 10th of June the Mission party, with Mr. Hastie and two German botanists who had joined it at Mauritius, arrived at the capital and were received with great kindness and courtesy. The king granted a good house in a large enclosure for the residence of Mr. Jeffreys and gave a piece of land where the artisans might establish themselves and carry out their handicrafts. A servant was apportioned to each of them, on condition that eight youths were properly instructed by them in their arts. The German botanists were placed in charge of the king's garden, having ten men and two boys under them with orders to utilise any piece of ground they might choose in cultivating plants and seeds of foreign and home growth.

Very soon a third school was opened with twelve pupils, under the care of Mr. Jeffreys, but in the midst of so much to encourage, the Mission band was saddened by the sudden death of Mr. Brooks, one of the artisans, ten days after his arrival at Antananarivo. He was buried in a grave granted by the king, who also gave permission for the ground surrounding it for a considerable distance to be walled in, and which became the general burial-place for the Christians of the capital.

The work of the missionaries entailed other anxieties. Jealousies were aroused in the minds of some of the people as to the object of the education of the young, and rumours were circulated that the white men intended to kidnap the children and carry them away to their own land. Some parents to preserve their children from going to the Mission schools hid them in rice holes, and several of them died of suffocation in these underground store-rooms. During this crisis Radama was absent prosecuting a war in the Sakalàva province, but his mother, who was a woman of great spirit, had it announced that all who published false reports of the missionaries, or who used methods of concealing their children so as to cause them to die, should be put to death. Thus an end was promptly made of these groundless rumours and of the ill-treatment of the children.

In July, 1822, the people brought in quantities of timber from the forest, and set to work on the erection of the house for Mr. Griffiths and the premises for church and school purposes. This was the largest building ever put up in the capital, and it excited great wonder and interest among the people.

In September, the members of the Mission formed themselves into a church. They adopted the Congregational pattern, but they arranged a basis of church membership of so broad a character as to comprehend Christians of every creed who might come to reside in the country. Then for the first time the Lord's Supper was observed among them.

As the work of the Mission assumed greater magnitude, the missionaries felt increasingly the need of becoming acquainted with the language of the country. They had begun by teaching their pupils English, and had succeeded so well that in 1822 the scholars were able in the presence of the king and his court to read the seventh chapter of the Acts of the Apostles in English, and then to translate it into Malagasy. From their pupils the missionaries were learning sounds and names of the native language, but their means of acquiring any knowledge were simply oral.

As already stated, no alphabet, grammar or dictionary of Malagasy was in existence. They had therefore the difficult work of learning, constructing and teaching the language at the same time. Very heroically did they struggle with the difficulty. They used the English letters as far as possible to express the native sounds, they gave the French pronunciation to the vowels, and they adopted Arabic numerals. In this formation of a written language for his nation the king took the deepest interest. He was learning both the English and French languages himself, and to simplify matters for his people he issued an order that no vowel was to have more than one sound. In two years' time, the missionaries succeeded in fixing the Malagasy alphabet, which has continued in use by both natives and foreigners to the present time.

In 1823 an adult school was formed in the courtyard of the royal palace, which was attended by three hundred officers of the army and their wives. Radama was moved to establish this school by hearing it said that there was no nation which could not read or write except the Malagasy and the Mozambiques. He replied, "Then I would rather not be a king at all than be king of such a people." From this time he devoted himself more than ever to promulgate means for having his people instructed. Towards the end of the year the missionaries arranged for the establishment of schools in districts away from the capital, and some of the most advanced of their pupils were placed in charge of them.

The new mission buildings were completed in December, and Divine service was held in them on the last Sunday of the year. The natives showed a great reluctance in attending the public preaching of the Word of God. The missionaries had their faith severely tried in witnessing, notwithstanding all their success in education and in diffusing a knowledge of useful arts, how the people clung to their old superstitions and showed utter indifference to Divine truth. Some were angry that the national idols should be slighted, while others stood in awe of the diviners and sorcerers, but Radama shook himself free from idolatry in a remarkable manner. When the people of a certain village asked him for a piece of scarlet cloth for their idol, he said: "Surely he must be very poor if he cannot obtain a piece of cloth for himself. If he be a god he can provide his own garments."

Since schools had been opened in the country districts the missionaries divided the Sundays between visiting them and preaching in the large hall or chapel recently opened, and they were greatly cheered by the increasing numbers who were drawn to listen to their addresses. At times more than a thousand were assembled, and members of the royal family were generally among them. The singing of the pupils was a great attraction in the services. The Malagasy are a musical people, and the missionaries had taken great pains to train the scholars in singing. The hymns thus taught were constantly heard in the homes, the streets, the fields, and indeed everywhere.

The officer left in charge of the capital when Radama was absent on his warlike expeditions took deep interest in the progress of the Mission work, and especially in the schools. He attended the public examination of the scholars in 1828, when the one small school commenced in Mr. Jones' room with three scholars had increased to thirty-two schools with four thousand young people. The governor addressed the assembly on this occasion, reminding his countrymen of the great obligations they were under to the white men, and urging on both old

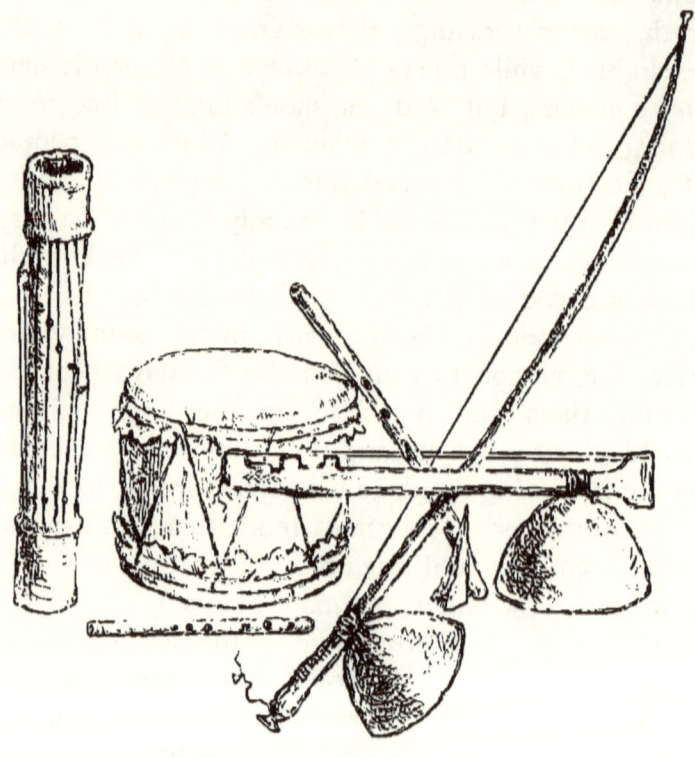

MALAGASY MUSICAL INSTRUMENTS.

and young the duty of encouraging them in their work.

A great trial befell the Mission in 1825 in the death of Rev. J. Jeffreys. He had been in the island three years, and had passed the last year at Ambatomanga, having charge of a school there and visiting the district around to make known the Gospel. Mrs. Jeffreys was taken ill, and it was deemed necessary to remove her to Mauritius, and in June Mr. Jeffreys sailed for Tamatave with her and his children. On the voyage he and his eldest daughter were seized with alarming symptoms, which speedily became aggravated. The child died in the arms of a sick mother when the father was too ill to be told of her danger, and in a few days the father followed the child, using his last breath in imparting comfort to his afflicted partner. Mrs. Jeffreys reached Mauritius, and after staying there six weeks sailed for England.

Immediately on hearing of the death of Mr. Jeffreys the London Missionary Society sent out Rev. David Johns to succeed him. He arrived at Antananarivo in due time, having with him his wife, Mr. and Mrs. Cameron, and Mr. and Mrs. Cummins, and Raolombelona, one of the youths sent to England by Radama, who had been taught the art of spinning and dyeing cotton at Manchester. Several of these youths had previously returned to Madagascar, and were busily engaged with the artisans in practising and teaching the industrial arts, and two of them still remained in England.

Another severe trial to the Mission came in the sudden death of the English Ambassador, Mr. James Hastie. This excellent man had been a firm friend and useful helper of the missionaries from their entrance into the island. He had experienced a succession of accidents which reduced his strength, and which brought on an attack of Malagasy fever accompanied by inflammation. He died on the 8th of October, to the deep regret of the king, who said: " I have lost many of my people, many of my soldiers, most of my officers, and several of my highest nobles, but all is nothing in comparison with this," and to the great distress of the missionaries, who mourned the loss of a true friend and wise counsellor. He had introduced them to the capital and to the king, he had succeeded by his discreet conduct in abolishing the slave trade, and he had done much to aid in the spread of civilisation, and the establishment of Christianity in the island.

On the 20th of October, 1826, his corpse was taken to the chapel, and a funeral service conducted by the Rev. D. Griffiths. Then the king and all the royal family, the judges, officers, Mission agents and others proceeded to the burial-ground, and the body was consigned to its resting-place by Rev. D. Jones.

When Radama returned from his wars, and was told of the troubles which had arisen concerning the children attending the schools, referred to in a previous page, he desired the missionaries not to move so fast, or they might endanger the peace and safety of his kingdom. When this became known the attendance of the children for a time fell off. In this difficulty the missionaries had recourse to prayer, and instituted meetings for this purpose to which many of the scholars came. These meetings spread to the country districts, and soon many of the young natives were heard simply and earnestly seeking the Divine blessing on their countrymen. The hearts of the missionaries were inspired with new courage, and the meetings became a happy training ground for spiritual exercises which bore fruit in later days.

A great forward step was taken in the operations of the Mission in 1826 by the introduction of a printing press, the first ever seen in the island. The king was delighted to have it at work in his capital, and set six youths apart to learn the art of printing. The press was brought out by a skilled printer, but two days after his arrival he was seized with the cruel fever of the country, and to the sorrow of the Christian band, after a short illness, he died.

The next year the Rev. J. J. Freeman came out to help in the work, accompanied by Mr. and Mrs. Canham. Radama was at Tamatave when they arrived and went to the shore to meet and welcome them. The missionaries, although they knew nothing of the working of a printing press by experience, resolved to attempt to issue a series of small guide books, and they succeeded so far beyond their expectation as to be encouraged to proceed to print books of greater bulk. A large portion of the Bible had been rendered in Malagasy by Messrs. Jones and Griffith, and they now set about a careful revision of their work preparatory to printing it. On the 1st of January, 1828, they passed through the press the first sheet of the Gospel of St. Luke, desiring, as they said: "To hallow the new year of our missionary labours by this service in opening the fountain of living waters in the midst of this parched ground, and with prayer that the healing streams may transform the wilderness into the garden of the Lord."

Up to this time the missionaries had not been cheered by any clear evidences of conversion to God, or any application for baptism by the natives. There were signs now apparent that some of their pupils and hearers were becoming ripe for making a public confession of faith in Christ. Before such a step could be taken it was deemed advisable to obtain the sanction of Radama, and Mr. Jones fully explained to him the nature of the ordinance. Soon afterwards he sent a message to the effect that he desired those whose time in the schools had expired to continue under instruction and to attend the services for worship, intimating also that as to being married or baptised, it was left to each person to judge and act for himself.

In order to further instruct those who had left the schools, and to fit those who were teaching in the villages for their work, an advanced course of lectures on the doctrines of the Bible was given by the missionaries in the head school of Antananarivo, and earnest care was taken in delivering the addresses to impress the consciences of the hearers with the practical bearings of the great truths expounded.

In 1828 a deputation from the London Missionary Society, consisting of Rev. D. Tyerman and G. Bennet, Esq., arrived at Tamatave. They had been on a missionary tour of inspection to the South Sea Islands, and other parts of the world, and now came to view the work of God in Madagascar. Mr. Jones went to Tamatave to meet and conduct them over the long journey of three hundred miles up the country. They were met by Mr. Freeman and other members of the Mission at Ambodinangavo, and so attended entered the capital. They had only time to take a brief survey of the operations of the missionaries when death struck Mr. Tyerman, and amidst much grief and disappointment his body was laid to rest in the Christian burial-ground.

But a far sadder event was about to occur which was full of eventful consequences to the nation, and

INTRODUCTION OF CHRISTIANITY. 45

especially to the future of Christianity in the country. The health of Radama had been rapidly failing for about a year. His constitution had never been robust, although his temperament was restless and vigorous. His strength had been exhausted, partly by camp life and attacks of fever, but more still by intemperance and indulgence in sensual vices. For several months before his end he scarcely was able to transact public business, and was only seen by a few intimate attendants and friends. He died on the 27th of June, 1828, at the early age of thirty-six years. Two days before he passed away Mr. Jones saw him but he was so exhausted that the few words he muttered could not be understood.

Madagascar never had a prince equal to him in all respects, and no one ever did so much toward the improvement of the people and the country. By his conquests in war he brought most of the Malagasy tribes into subjection to himself. By his alliances with western nations he gave much encouragement to commerce and to the growth of the people in civilisation, and although he never became a Christian, he had throughout been a warm friend to the missionaries, and to the establishment of Christianity. His suppression of the slave trade, his adoption of a system of education, his introduction of useful industries and arts, the reduction of the Malagasy language to writing, and the introduction of printing, but especially the proclamation of the Gospel in the island, all make his reign one of unsurpassed importance to the nation.

The way in which he shook off the superstitions of witchcraft and idolatry and laboured to destroy heathendom showed him to be a man of great breadth of mind, and had he been as virtuous as he was able, his life might have been prolonged, and become an unspeakable blessing to the people.

That such a man should be struck down at a time when his presence seemed to be imperatively needful for the completion of reforms he had initiated and measures he was planning, seemed to be a mysterious dispensation of Providence, and the Mission was now to enter upon a chequered history of repression and persecution, and then upon a course of triumphant success.

CHAPTER III.

THE GOSPEL ROOTING ITSELF—GATHERING STORM.

"Oh! let all the soul within you, for the truth's sake go abroad!
Strike! let every nerve and sinew tell on ages—tell for God.
Sealed to blush, to waver, never; crossed, baptised, and born again,
Sworn to be Christ's soldiers ever, Oh, for Christ at least be men." *A. C. Coxe.*

THE friends who attended Radama in his last moments were bewildered by his death, and in their suspense resolved to keep the event secret until they had duly decided on the course of conduct they ought to adopt. The royal band therefore played each afternoon in the palace-yard, and announcements were made that the king was improving. This deceitful policy was fraught with danger, and produced great mischief to the State. Radama had no son living, and had adopted as his successor Rakatobe the son of Prince Ratefy. He was an amiable and intelligent youth. He was the first scholar who entered the Mission School eight years before, and was a warm friend to the missionaries. Indeed, he left ground for believing that he had been really converted by the grace of God, and become a believer in Jesus Christ.

Instead of at once proclaiming Rakatobe king, his friends dallied and delayed until it was too late. A young officer who was in the secret informed Ranavalona, one of Radama's wives, of the true state of affairs. She was by no means a favourite with the king, but she was a bold and ambitious woman. She sent for two officers who were devoted to her interests, and promised them high promotion in the army if they would conspire to make her queen. This could only be done by much bloodshed, indeed, by the complete cutting-off of Radama's relations. She thought nothing of this, but was quite willing to "wade through slaughter to a throne." The officers who espoused her cause won over to her interests a number of officials and a portion of the troops. The young Prince Rakatobe was seized in the middle of a certain night by Ranavalona's emissaries and carried out to a considerable distance from the capital. There he was placed on the brink of a newly prepared grave. He pleaded for a few moments' respite, which his murderers reluctantly granted. These were spent in fervent prayer to God, and then he was ruthlessly speared, and his body buried in the earth.

The measures of Ranavalona were taken with combined caution and promptitude. Like Athaliah of old, she "rose up and destroyed all the seed royal." On the 1st of August, the troops pledged to her service were marched into the palace-yard. The priests and supporters of idolatry were already gathered there. An announcement was then made that "the idols" had named Ranavalona as the proper occupant of the

GOSPEL ROOTING ITSELF—GATHERING STORM. 49

throne, and allegiance was commanded to be offered to her. Some of Radama's adherents boldly spoke out and declared that Rakatobe, the late king's nephew, and after him Rakataka his daughter should fill the throne, but while they yet spoke a signal was given and they were speared by the soldiery. After this no further opposition was heard. Ranavalona was declared queen, and the welkin rang with the roar of cannon and the shouts of the people.

After this there came the shameful murder of Prince Ratefy and his amiable wife, of Radama's brothers and uncle, and of all his early and faithful companions. His mother also was sent to prison and starved to death. A period of mourning was ordained for the late king, and all amusements were forbidden. As the new Government considered the teaching in the mission schools and all mission work to belong to this category, the missionaries devoted themselves diligently to the translation of the New Testament, and the composition of books of a simple character on several useful subjects. A competent printer had been sent out from England to replace the first who had died, and the Government permitted a number of youths to be employed in copying manuscripts and in working the press.

Six months after Radama's death, the Government allowed the mission schools to be re-opened in villages where no idols were kept, but seven hundred teachers and scholars from these schools were suddenly drafted as soldiers, a step which tended to confirm the uneasiness which existed in the minds of the parents as to the ultimate purpose of educating the children. Thus the attendance was reduced to less than one-half of what it had previously been. Shortly after this Mr. Lyall,

D

the English envoy in succession to Mr. Hastie, was dismissed from the Court, as the queen announced that she did not hold herself to be bound by the treaty entered into between Radama and the British Govern-

THE QUEEN'S PALACE, ANTANANARIVO.

ment. She also declined to receive the annual subsidy paid for compensation for the loss of the slave trade.

On the 12th of June, 1829, an assembly of about sixty thousand people was gathered to witness the

GOSPEL ROOTING ITSELF—GATHERING STORM.

coronation of Ranavalona. She stood upon a traditional sacred stone while the ceremonial of consecration was performed. She took two of the national idols in her hand, and said: "My predecessors have given you to me; I put my trust in you, therefore support me." Then she gave an address to the multitude, declaring that her ancestors had received the kingdom by the authority of the gods, and that it had come to Radama on condition that she should be his successor.

In the month of August alarming rumours reached the capital that the French were meditating a descent upon the island, and in October six war vessels came to Tamatave, and landed a strong armed force upon the shore. They speedily took possession of the town, and from thence made sallies in various directions, defeating all opposition, and doing much damage. The queen sent envoys to confer with the commander, and the negotiations were so prolonged that the Malagasy fever had sufficient time to accomplish what the warriors might not have done, and only a small remnant who survived sailed away from the plague-haunted coast. Various threats of a speedy return were held out from time to time, but they were never carried into execution.

This attack on the part of the French aroused the Government to the necessity of strengthening the defences of the island. An appeal was made to the idols for protection; old superstitions were revived, and diviners became the chief advisers of the queen. All this boded no good to the Christians. The missionaries were only allowed to work within narrow limits; the supporters of idolatry sought to impede their operations in many ways, and all encouragement of education was withdrawn.

Mr. Freeman was so convinced that no good could be accomplished under existing circumstances that he and his family left the island to visit Mauritius. Unfortunately, as they travelled to the coast, his infant son caught the prevalent fever, and died shortly after being taken on board.

Suddenly a more friendly disposition was manifested towards the missionaries and their work. This was due to the fear inspired by the late French invasion, and the expectation of its renewal; also to the increasing value of the English artisans in diffusing a knowledge of the industrial arts. Fuller liberty to preach and teach was therefore given, and the work of translating and printing was pushed forward with the utmost vigour. Thus, the missionaries hoped to be able to leaven the public mind with Christian sentiment, and to prevent much evil which was threatening to come to the Mission.

In March, 1830, it was the delight of the translators to issue an edition of 5000 copies of the New Testament in the Malagasy language. They had already issued 1000 copies of various tracts, 1500 catechisms, and 2000 spelling-books. They also sent out thousands of copies of parts of the New Testament. Thus a commencement of Malagasy literature was made; not by the wise, the disputer, or the critic, but by the humble preachers of the cross of Christ. The books were read by great numbers, not only in the capital, but in distant provinces by those who had formerly been mission scholars. No doubt it was partly due to the reading of the New Testament among the natives that the attendance at Divine worship greatly increased during this year.

Mr. Jones, the founder of the Mission, had suffered from a severe illness, and resolved to return to England to seek the restoration of his health. He had laboured earnestly for the establishment of Christianity in the island, and had won unbounded confidence from his companions. On leaving the capital, the queen, the Government, multitudes of the people, and his fellow-Christians all vied with each other in testifying their respect for him. A salute was fired as he left the capital, and the queen allowed him a guard of twenty men to go with him to the coast. He sailed to Mauritius, and thence to England, where he arrived on the 29th of June, 1831.

The missionaries rapidly pushed forward the translation of the Old Testament, and published the books separately as they were finished. They also were called upon to issue new and enlarged editions of the spelling-book and similar hand-books. But they were most cheered by the earnestness manifested by the people in attending the preaching of the Word. The chapel in which Mr. Griffiths ministered was crowded, and many could not get in. The people pressed as inquirers to the houses of the missionaries, and many showed by their pure and consistent lives that a great change had taken place in them. In order to meet the growing demand for accommodation, a good and convenient chapel was erected at Ambatonakanga, in the northern part of the capital. It was opened for worship on the 5th of June, 1831, and was at once filled with a devout congregation, who listened to the ministry of Mr. Johns with great avidity. The artisans also found their work being constantly more highly prized. Mr. Cameron, who was at the head of the machine shops, had six hundred youths under training, and both he and his fellow-craftsmen laboured assiduously for the highest welfare of those who were under their care.

At last the faith and prayer expended on the Mission for so many years were to be rewarded by tangible results of the most blessed kind. Several natives professed to be converted, and desired to be baptised. Inquiries were made of the Government as to its willingness to permit the rite to be administered, and the queen sent a message to the effect that she did not wish to interfere with the consent previously given by King Radama. Therefore, on Sunday, the 29th of May, 1831, twenty converts were publicly baptised by Mr. Griffiths before a deeply impressed audience. On the following Sunday eight were baptised in the newly opened chapel by Mr. Johns, six of whom were young men, who afterwards became preachers and teachers of the Gospel to their countrymen.

Petty persecution and spiteful annoyances were speedily directed against those who had thus professed Christianity, and contemptuous epithets were applied to them by their heathen neighbours. All these were patiently endured, and the native Christians sought earnestly to secure the conversion of their opponents. With this end in view they held frequent meetings in their own houses for reading the Bible and prayer. Through these and other efforts the number of believers multiplied, and by the end of the year there were seventy enrolled in one church alone, and several members of the royal family and Government officials professed faith in Christ and desired to be baptised. But on the day before the rite was to be observed, a note of disapproval was sent them from the queen, and it was deemed advisable to defer the service for a time.

During the reign of Radama, a law had been passed forbidding the use of wine or spirituous liquors in Imerina. It was not strictly obeyed, but advantage was taken of it by the heathen party to harass the Christians. The Lord's Supper had been observed for the first time by the members, when the queen sent a message that the law of the country forbade the use of wine by natives. The missionaries therefore resolved to use water instead of wine at the ordinance. Shortly after this an order was issued by the Government forbidding all scholars who were receiving instruction by its authority, and all soldiers in the army to join the Church or receive baptism. Those who had already united with the Church were forbidden to receive the Lord's Supper in future. On the next communion Sabbath, the soldiers present in the service abstained from partaking of the elements, but with evident distress of mind. From this time no Government pupil or soldier was permitted to unite with the Church.

A forward movement in the history of the Mission was now taken by the organisation of a Christian church at Ambodinandohalo. A declaration of faith of a catholic character was agreed upon, the form of church government was a mixture of Congregationalism and Presbyterianism, and the believers assembled gave each other the right hand of fellowship and pledged themselves to promote the spiritual welfare and interest of each other in every possible way. The prospect at this time was so bright before the missionaries that they resolved to invite Mr. Freeman, then labouring at the Cape of Good Hope, to resume his labours among them. On the 29th of August, Mr. Freeman accompanied by Mr. and Mrs. Atkinson, who had been working on the African Mission, arrived at Tamatave. They brought with them a number of horses, sheep, and other animals, with many plants, roots, and seeds, which they hoped to cultivate on the island. On the arrival of the party, they were welcomed at Tamatave by two of the missionary artisans who had come down from the capital to inform them of the state of the Mission, and who also brought a message from the queen that the missionaries and all their stores were to be sent to Antananarivo free of expense. Permission was given to Mr. and Mrs. Atkinson to remain twelve months in the island.

Other signs of encouragement occurred at this time which gave the missionaries hope that the work of God was about to prosper gloriously. At the general examination of the schools the queen sent an order for the scholars to attend regularly the teaching of the Christian agents; on the completion of the cutting of a canal, an important work carried out by the artisans, she sent a message expressing the great obligation the nation was under to the Mission, and thus a prospect of the wide extension of the Gospel seemed to be opening out.

But all this favour was only temporary, and was like the flash of light which sometimes precedes the darkening cloud and the destructive tempest. To-

GOSPEL ROOTING ITSELF—GATHERING STORM. 57

wards the close of the year an order was received from the Government prohibiting the administration of the rites of baptism and the Lord's Supper; officers in the army who had professed Christianity or were favourable to it were degraded to a lower rank, and attempts were made to divest the education imparted in the numerous schools of any religious character. Mr. and Mrs. Atkinson, who were giving valuable service in the cause of education, were informed that they must leave the island at the end of the year. The English Christians saw clearly that they were only allowed to work on sufferance, and that their presence was only permitted because of the impulse they were giving to civilisation and education. They redoubled their exertions to pour a true religious literature upon the people, and to instruct them in the public services, and they were greatly stimulated by the increasing solicitude with which the people both pressed to listen to them, and desired the books which passed through their press. Not less than 21,000 copies of various publications were issued in the course of the year.

In 1832 the first death among the converts occurred. It was that of Rabenohaja, a poor slave whose business it was to attend his young master to school; and in so doing, he learnt also to read. By careful reading of the New Testament he had been led to believe in Christ, and was one of the first natives to express a desire for baptism. It may here be said that in baptising the natives the missionaries did not encourage them to take new names, but simply asked them to pronounce their names before baptism, and then performed the rite without further questioning.

When Rabenohaja was asked his name, he replied, "Ra-poor-negro." Mr. Griffiths being surprised, asked him again, but he answered, "Yes, that is the name I wish to take," and he was forthwith baptised in it. When he was afterwards asked why he assumed so singular a name, he said: "Oh, I had seen in your printing office the tract of The Poor Negro with a woodcut representing him with his knees bended and his eyes lifted up to heaven, and I thought, being a slave like him, there was nothing I so much desired as to become like him in spirit, and therefore I took his name."

He showed great earnestness from this time in the study of the Bible; he had the greatest enjoyment in all religious exercises, and became of great service to his own class. Not long after his baptism he was seized with Malagasy fever and was cut off by it. Sorrow, darkness, and despair are the usual attendants of death in Madagascar, but this first trophy of the Gospel who went home to heaven from there was filled with perfect peace. "I am going to Jehovah Jesus," he said; "Jesus is fetching me. I do not fear; I do not fear."

The queen and her followers who had usurped the government of Madagascar on the death of Radama were not left undisturbed in the exercise of their authority. A large force of Sakalàvas gathered in the district west of the capital with the object of invading the province of Imerina. The Government sent a large body of troops against them but no battle took place. In 1831 an army had been sent to attack the southern provinces, under the command of the chief officer, who was a bigoted supporter of the ancient idols.

Before the host left Antananarivo a great ceremonial was held for the purpose of securing the protection of Rakelimalaza, one of the national idols. The idol was carried through the lines of soldiers, followed by priests, who sprinkled them with so called sacred water as they passed. This, they were told, would keep them from harm and secure them success. The Christians in the army begged to be absent from the ceremony, as they could not conscientiously countenance it. The general consented to their absence, but said the idol would be revenged upon them.

The army then marched to the scene of warfare. It was divided into three parts. The largest division was led by the general, and the idol was carried with it, so as to give it special protection and success. It was a remarkable thing that in this campaign this section suffered the severest defeat and lost the largest number of lives. The division containing the Christian soldiers was placed in the most dangerous positions and was preserved almost intact. The Christians distinguished themselves by their kindness towards their captives and their purity of life. They held frequent meetings for praise and prayer during the war, and when the campaign was over they were able to report to the missionaries that many of their comrades had been won from idolatry to the faith of Jesus.

Other raids were made by the Government upon weaker tribes, and immense numbers of lives were sacrificed in these wars. Then reports were circulated that the French were returning to the island, and every teacher and scholar above the age of thirteen was drafted for the army. This made parents more reluctant than ever to send their children to the schools, and many of them purchased young slaves and sent them as substitutes for their own children. By this artifice the slaves were drafted into the army and the children of the parents were left at home. About three thousand pupils were withdrawn from the Mission schools by this action of the Government. The work of the Mission was by no means lost, for the pupils carried with them not only the advantages of secular knowledge but the careful training in godliness which had always been the chief object of the missionaries. About 15,000 pupils had passed through the schools, and many of these had taught members of their own families to read, so that probably not less than double that number were now able to read the Word of God in their own language. At this time the British and Foreign Bible Society and the Religious Tract Society made large donations to supply these readers with the Bible and other useful books.

The missionaries now sought a wider diffusion of the Gospel and took frequent journeys into the country, preaching to large numbers of people. Very many renounced their idols and became disciples of Christ. They cast away their charms and burnt their idols. Among the idols renounced was one which had been a great source of income to its possessor. It belonged to the chief of the district and had been in his family for several generations. It was a most miserable object. It consisted of a piece of wood, circular in form, seven inches long, and three-quarters of an inch broad. This was surrounded by six short pieces of wood and six hollow silver ornaments, shaped like crocodiles' teeth. Three pieces of wood were placed on one side and three on the other side, the silver ornaments being placed between them. These were filled with sacred oil to be used in the consecration of charms and other objects of superstition. Sometimes the silver ornaments were detached from the idol, filled with pieces of wood, and worn by persons who were going to war or travelling through a plague-haunted district. Small square pieces of wood were strung like beads on a string and attached to the idol or worn by the persons who carried the silver ornaments. The chief who owned this idol had two sons in the army, and to one of them he intrusted these small pieces of holy wood, to be sold to those who wished to be preserved from all danger in war or pestilence. Such virtue was supposed to rest in these bits of wood that often a couple of sheep or goats or bullocks would be given for one of them.

In 1832 Mr. Johns visited the village where this idol was kept. He spent much time with the chief who owned it, and on departing he cordially invited the young officer who had charge of the sale of the wooden charms to visit him in Antananarivo. The invitation was accepted, and in the capital Mr. Johns had serious conversation with him and gave him a copy of the New Testament. He carefully read the book and had conversations with Mr. Johns until he became convinced of the foolishness of idolatry and turned with simple earnest faith to the Lord Jesus. The young convert now sought to persuade his relatives to abandon their superstitions, and succeeded with several of them. His parents, however, mourned over his conduct because he now refused to sell the charms which had been so great a source of wealth to them. The heathen party had all its persecuting instincts aroused by the conversion of this young officer and he was accused before the queen of being guilty of witchcraft. He was condemned to pass through the ordeal of drinking the tangena water. Some of his friends tried to induce him to appeal to

MALAGASY IDOL.

divination for a favourable issue, but he refused and boldly committed himself to the will of God. He drank the poison water and passed the trial successfully. He quickly recovered from the effects of it, and his restoration so impressed his family that their confidence in the idol was completely shaken, they became sincere Christians, the idol was given up to the missionary, and it is now preserved in the Museum of the London Missionary Society. The young officer remained a humble and useful Christian and died a peaceful death about the close of the year 1833.

Another interesting instance of the giving up of idols is recorded about this time. A husband and wife had ordered from a maker of idols a household god. On the day appointed they went to receive it, but it was not ready, and they had to wait for it till the evening. The idol-maker went to the forest, selected a piece of wood, made the idol and left the fragments of his work scattered near the fire-place. The visitors were invited to share his evening meal and he used the fragments of the idol wood to boil his rice. They paid for their treasure and returned home. Soon afterwards a Christian friend visited them and read the Scriptures to them. Amongst other words he read Isaiah xliv. 16, 17, "with part he roasteth roast, maketh a fire, warmeth himself, and the residue thereof he maketh a god." The woman was startled and impressed by the exact description of what had taken place at the idol-maker's, and abandoning idol worship she became a follower of Jesus.

At the end of 1834 the Mission looked brighter in prospects than ever. In the capital two hundred persons had joined the Church, many were attending classes for the study of the Bible, and crowds came to the public services. Many meetings were also held in towns and villages ranging over a district of one hundred miles round, and a large distribution of the Scriptures was made in those places. The Government entered into a new engagement with Mr. Cameron, the principal of the machine shops, and thus hope was given that for some years the work of the Mission would not be interfered with.

But very quickly the sky darkened and clouds of ominous blackness overspread the horizon. The first indication of persecution was an order from the queen that no one should learn to read or write save in the

OPEN-AIR PREACHING.

schools established by the Government. Early in 1835 it was evident that some further discouragement was to be given to the Mission by the jubilant tone of the supporters of heathenism. The queen's chief advisers were three brothers, who were in league to do all they could to suppress Christianity, and they recognised that the time had now come when a decisive blow might be aimed at it. These officers had several relatives who were members of the Christian Church, among whom was a nephew who was the keeper of the national idols. In January this young man was told by one of his uncles, who had adopted him as his son, that at an approaching festival the queen would present a bullock to the chief idol, and that he would be expected both to offer sacrifice to it and afterwards to eat a portion of the meat sacrificed. He firmly declined to do this, and the chiefs were greatly enraged not only against the young man, but against the faith which inspired him to disobey the mandate.

Soon after this a Christian was observed to be at work on a day which was reckoned as sacred to the idols, and he declared to his friends that faith in such things was useless and wicked. A complaint was presented to the queen against him, and charges were made at the same time against the Christians—that they made light of the ancient gods, that they offered prayer to their own God, but especially that their women refused to practise the immorality which was general among the women of the island. The man was ordered to undergo the trial by tangena water, which he did successfully. The anger of the queen however burned as fiercely as ever.

Shortly after this the queen was sick and the chief officer of the Government was sent to the idol for a powerful charm which it was said would restore her. Some of his relatives who were Christians spoke to him of the true God who alone could heal and restore, affirming that the idol and its charms could effect no cure. The queen, on being told of this, expressed much displeasure; and a few days afterwards, on passing one of the churches, and hearing the members singing, she exclaimed: "They will not stop till some of them lose their heads."

The Christians were fully alive to the seriousness of the crisis. They sought to avoid every occasion of offence, but fortified themselves by much prayer to endure hardship as good soldiers. Their enemies daily plied the queen with stories of them calculated to lead her to conclude that they were labouring to undermine her throne and authority. Still the numbers who thronged to listen to the preaching of the Gospel and to unite with the Church were greater than ever.

One day a chief of the highest rank came in to the queen and said: "I want a spear, a bright and sharp one; grant my request!" He was asked the reason for such a demand and he answered that he had observed the rapid growth of the Christians, that he was assured they aimed at subverting the old system of religion entirely, and he desired to plunge the spear to his heart ere the evil day came.

This so much aroused the queen that she declared she would destroy Christianity, if it cost the life of every Christian in the island. For a fortnight there was profound silence in the palace—no music, or games, or reading—but a deep solemn stillness, which rested heavily upon every one as a presage of the coming storm.

On the 26th of February the missionaries and other Englishmen were summoned to the palace to receive a message from the sovereign. It was to the effect that, while she thanked them for the good services they had rendered to the country, and while they were at liberty to follow their own religious customs, she would not permit her subjects to depart from their old national customs, and that in future she would not allow them to practise baptism, or keep the Sabbath, or remain members of the Christian churches. She gave full permission for the teaching of the arts or sciences, but not religion. The missionaries sent a petition earnestly entreating her not to suppress their meetings, or prevent their work, but to continue to her subjects the religious liberty they had so long enjoyed. To this a reply was speedily sent, declaring that the queen firmly adhered to her decision.

On the 1st of March a great assembly of the people was held at Antananarivo. Not less than 150,000 people were estimated to be present. The day was ushered in by the firing of cannon, to give it special importance. Fifteen thousand soldiers were assembled with the view of showing the determination of Ranavalona to enforce her decree. An edict was read, forbidding anyone to refuse to worship the idols, and observe the old customs of the land; also prohibiting Christian baptism, the observance of the Lord's Supper and the Sabbath, and requiring all persons who had become Christians to report themselves at the palace within a month. If they failed to thus confess and accuse themselves, and were informed against by others, they would surely be put to death.

A deep silence followed the reading of the message, which was broken by some prominent chiefs remonstrating against its severity, and proposing to present a peace-offering to Ranavalona on condition that it should be modified so as not to pry into the past, and that it should not require self-accusation. The judges promised to consult the queen, and return an answer on the following day. On the morrow an immense multitude again assembled. They were informed that the queen adhered to her decision; but that instead of a month, only one week would be allowed for the self-accusation, and that further expostulation was forbidden. An order was sent to the missionaries to abandon all religious teaching, but permitting the continuance of lessons in science by Mr. Cameron. All the pupils in the schools, numbering several hundreds, led by twelve senior teachers, attended at the palace to accuse themselves. They were deeply affected, and many of them had determined to suffer death rather than return to the worship of idols.

After several days had been spent in hearing confessions, an edict was published, degrading about four hundred who had held office under the queen or the Government to one-third of their rank and income. Those who held no office were fined according to the measure of their Christian practice. There was scarcely a family in or near Antananarivo which was not to some extent involved in the accusations, and the greatest consternation generally prevailed during the days of this awful week. The practice of Christianity was artfully represented to the queen as being treasonable to her, and defiant of the ancient customs, and she was incited to commence the shedding of blood. The great body of the believers stood bravely to their faith and gave themselves unceasingly to prayer. A few were appalled by the prospect of punishment, and apostatised by either plunging into sin, or denying ever having believed in Christ. These were a few tares in a beautiful harvest field.

There were some signal examples of bravery and fortitude among the natives. One prominent member declared before the judges that during nearly four years he had prayed several times each day, confessing his sins, imploring Divine help to live well, seeking blessings upon his family, his friends, the queen, and the country. He earnestly exhorted the judges to believe in Jesus. He was listened to with great attention, and was assured that his prayers were good, but they were opposed to the will of the queen, and must be given up. Companies of Christians met at midnight to pray in secret. One such meeting was held in the vestry of the church at Ambatonakanga ; and one night an officer of high rank came in, and declared he was so grieved at the injustice of the Government that he had determined to join the persecuted band. This man became a noble follower of Christ and a true friend of the Christians in the time of trouble.

The missionaries continued in every way possible to them to impart consolation and instruction to the afflicted churches ; but the risk was great, and much caution had to be exercised. Still, the converts were numerous, and the believers pressed to the Lord's Table, and eagerly drank in the preacher's word.

The great work of translating the whole Bible was finished by the unremitting and united labour of the missionaries, and Mr. Baker, the head of the missionary printers, with his assistants, printed off many copies. This was a boon only second to the introduction into the island of Christianity itself, and many people walked sixty and a hundred miles to obtain the volume. Following this

Messrs. Freeman and Johns compiled English and Malagasy dictionaries, which are in use to this day.

All aggressive mission work was now at an end. The Government would gladly have kept the artisans, especially the smiths and machinists, to carry on their useful secular work, but these men were Christians first and artisans second, and resolved to leave the country. In June Mr. Freeman, accompanied by Messrs. Cameron, Chick, and Kitching, left Antananarivo, leaving Messrs. Johns and Baker to hold the fort for a short time longer.

The year 1836 proved to be one of bitterest trial to the Mission. The Government, so far from being appeased by the departure of so many of the English Christians, became more severe. The servants of the remaining missionaries had to undergo the ordeal of the tangena, and several of them died from its effects. An infant born to one of them was killed by the queen's order when a day old, and the Sabbath was desecrated by compulsory work and low amusements.

Mr. Freeman occupied his time chiefly in the translation into Malagasy of the incomparable prose poem by the Tinker of Bedford Gaol, "The Pilgrim's Progress." The peculiar situation of the native Christians tended to make it a most attractive book to them, and the translator felt from his own position such living sympathy with his work as to transfuse it with much of the vigour and quaintness of the original. The Christians were obliged to exercise the greatest caution in recognising each other, and adopted a kind of spiritual freemasonry in doing so. For example, one would quote Jer. xxxviii. 15, "If I declare it unto thee, wilt thou not directly put me to death?" And in reply the following verse would be given:—"As the Lord liveth which made us this soul, I will not put thee to death, neither will I give thee unto the hands of those men who seek thy life." Like the early Christians who met in the sand caves of Rome, or the Covenanters who gathered on the mountains or in the forest glades of Scotland, the Malagasy met on the tops of hills or on extensive plains, and there sent up the strain of praise and prayer to the Eternal Father.

The remaining missionaries now received notice from the Government to follow their brethren. Their preparations for quitting the island were soon completed. They left with the native Christians about seventy Bibles, several boxes filled with copies of the Psalms, the New Testament and Hymn Books, and commending their afflicted flocks to God by fervent prayer, Messrs. Johns and Baker departed from the island in July, after a bright career of devoted service in the noblest of all causes.

CHAPTER IV.

THE NOBLE ARMY OF MARTYRS.

> "Their blood is shed
> In confirmation of the noblest claim,—
> Our claim to feed upon immortal truth,
> To walk with God, to be divinely free
> To soar and to anticipate the skies."—*Cowper*.

THE first special object of the persecution which was about to rage with bloodthirsty fierceness was a lady named Rafaravavy, who had become an earnest Christian during the life of King Radama. Her family had long been zealots in behalf of the old superstitions, but she had been led to Christ chiefly by means of a native Christian. She then took a large house in Antananarivo and consecrated it for the use of the Mission. In this house Rafaravavy and a group of friends met frequently for Bible reading and prayer, after the edict of Ranavalona was issued. Three of her slaves gave information of these meetings to the Government. When Rafaravavy heard of it she hid her Bibles and other Christian books and calmly waited the result. Her father, although a heathen, ordered the slaves to be fettered and imprisoned, but she liberated them, wept over them, freely forgave them, and spoke to them fervently as to the salvation of God. Two of them were won by her piety to the side of Christ, and one of them afterwards became a martyr.

When Rafaravavy was brought before the judges she was questioned as to the names of her companions. These she firmly refused to give. On this the queen ordered her to be at once put to death. Several high officials pleaded for her life on the ground of eminent services rendered to the state by her father and brother, and she was reprieved. In a few days an officer brought her the news that her sentence was commuted into a fine, but she was warned that if she offended again her life would be taken. On her release she was carefully watched by her enemies, and to avoid them she took a house at Ambatonakanga, and in it a party of Christians gathered, some of them coming many miles, to worship the God who had saved them.

About a year after this escape, two women went before the judges and informed against ten Christians who had met in the house of Rafaravavy for prayer. When the news was carried to the queen she swore, saying: " Then they shall die, for they despise my law." The persons accused were at once arrested. Officers visited Rafaravavy and requested her to discover her friends, telling her that the queen knew them, but she must tell the whole truth. The brave woman answered: " If the queen knows, why do you ask me?"

One of her associates who had confessed to having

prayed with her was brought and confronted with her. She boldly admitted it. She was asked where they had prayed, and said: " In our own houses and many other places." They asked if she had not prayed on a certain mountain? She said: "Yes, but not there only. Wherever we went we remembered God, in the house and out of it; in the town, the country, and on the mountains."

The other prisoners were closely examined, and a young woman named Rasalama being told that the others had given a full list of those concerned in the meeting, and that it would be to her benefit to do likewise, gave the names of seven more than those apprehended. Amongst these was Paul the aged diviner, previously mentioned as owning a famous idol, and the whole were at once arrested. When Paul was examined he fully admitted his crime. He said: " I have prayed to that God who created me and supports me, who is the source of all good, to make me a good man. I prayed that He would bless the queen and give her true happiness both in this world and the next. I asked Him to bless the officers and judges, and all the people so that there might be no more brigands or liars, and that God would make all the people wise and good." The officers were much impressed, and observed that there was no evil but good in such prayer, and there followed among themselves conversation as to the policy of punishing people for such conduct.

In fourteen days an order was issued to the people to pillage the house and property of Rafaravavy. They rushed into her dwelling, and carried off all it contained, afterwards pulling down and removing the materials of which the house was composed. Rafaravavy was led by four soldiers, who usually conducted executions, to the place where criminals were put to death. She thought her end was come, and in the words of Stephen she committed her soul to Christ. A Christian friend came near enough for her to speak to him, and she asked him to keep near her, so that if she had strength to bear testimony for Christ at the last, he could use it to encourage any who might have to suffer in like manner. On the way, she was taken into a house and fetters were placed upon her limbs. As the smith was riveting them upon her, one of the soldiers said: "Do not make them too fast, as it will be difficult to take them off, and she is to be executed at cock crow to-morrow morning."

But during that night a considerable portion of the capital was destroyed by fire, and the consternation caused by this event was so great that the execution of Rafaravavy was delayed. Rasalama, the woman who had been drawn into betraying seven of her comrades into the hands of their persecutors, was kept in confinement, and a relative informed her that the Government would not have known anything against those she had implicated but for her betrayal. She was overwhelmed with grief at the tidings, and expressed her surprise that those who were guilty of no fault should be subjected to severe punishment. She also declared that she had no fear when she was arrested, but rather was glad to be reckoned worthy to suffer for Christ, adding, "I have hope of life in heaven."

What Rasalama said was repeated to the commander-in-chief, who ordered her to be put in irons and to be beaten. She continued singing hymns and said to her tormentors: "My life shall go for my companions. You say, Rafaravavy will be put to death; but no, she will not die, I shall be killed instead of her." She was ordered to be executed the next morning, and in the meantime was kept in irons, which were fastened to her feet, hands, knees and neck, drawing her body into an agonising position.

On the morrow as they conveyed her to the place of execution she sang hymns of praise, and when she passed the Christian church, exclaimed, "There I heard the words of the Saviour." About a mile farther on she came to a broad ditch which was strewed with the bones of criminals previously executed. Here permission was given her to engage in prayer. She knelt upon the ground, and with calm and peaceful fortitude committed her soul into the hands of the Lord Jesus. Then the executioners hurled their spears, and the martyr spirit went home. Some of the bystanders scoffed, but many more were moved with pity. The executioners were led to remark on the charm there appeared to be in Christianity to take away the fear of death, and one Christian who was present exclaimed when reporting the event to his friends: "If I might die so tranquil and happy a death I would willingly suffer for the Saviour too." The execution took place on the 14th of August, 1837, and Rasalama was the first of a bright and numerous train of martyrs who gladly sealed their testimony for Jesus with their blood.

After this baptism of blood, the members of the Church under arrest, about two hundred in number, were condemned to perpetual slavery. The venerable Paul, who had been in fetters night and day for some time, became a slave with four fellow-Christians in the rice fields of the chief minister of the Government. They were fettered each night at the close of their work and lived together in a small hut. Here Paul comforted the hearts of his fellow-sufferers, especially reciting almost daily the words of the forty-sixth Psalm, which was his favourite portion of the Bible. Rafaravavy had also been kept in irons and carefully guarded by soldiers. The queen ordered that now she should be led into the market-place and offered for sale. She was bought by the chief military officer, and given into the care of one of his helpers, who treated her kindly and allowed her to go where she liked, so long as her apportioned work was well done. Her husband was an officer in the army, and he obtained leave of absence for some months in order to spend as much time with her as she could give from her daily task.

The next victim to the persecuting rage of the queen was Rafaralahy, a young man who had witnessed the execution of Rasalama. He had received the Christians into his house for worship, and a backslider from the faith secretly informed against him, and gave the names of twelve others who met with him for prayer. He was seized and heavily fettered. Attempts were made to force him to betray his companions, but he bravely refused, saying: "I am here, I have done it, let the queen do with me as she pleases; I will not betray my friends." In three days he was led to the place of execution. He earnestly exhorted his executioners to turn to Jesus, and assured them of his own happiness. He knelt and prayed for his country and for his associates, and then calmly gave himself over to God. The soldiers prepared to throw him on the ground according to their custom, but he forbade them and gently laid himself down. Then he was speared, and his spirit passed away. After this his persecutors seized his wife and servant; and bound and scourged them until their fortitude gave way, and they gave the names of those who had attended the meetings held in their house.

That day, when Rafaravavy was conversing with a few friends, all ignorant of the terrible cruelties which had been perpetrated, a note was put into her hand. As she read it her face changed, and she told her friends that Rafaralahy was killed, and they were betrayed. There was no safety for them but in flight, and Rafaravavy with two other women at once set off from the house. They went to the place of execution, united in prayer, then bade each other farewell and separated. Rafaravavy went into the capital and sought out four of her friends. They prayed together, sent a messenger to warn Paul and others, and at midnight fled from the place. That same evening the death warrant of Rafaravavy was issued. The next morning the officers in charge of it went to the house of her master and several other places to arrest her. They were unable to discover her, but the aged Paul and one of her nephews were seized and imprisoned. For a night and a day she and her friends travelled with all speed, nor did they stop until they reached the residence of friends forty miles west of Antananarivo where they were joyfully received.

For several months this little band of fugitives moved from place to place, sometimes hiding in the depths of the forest, and having to tap the traveller's tree for their support, sometimes finding shelter with

Christian friends, sometimes in imminent peril of discovery from bands of soldiers who were sent in pursuit of them.

One night Rafaravavy's hiding-place was reported to a band of pursuers, and they proceeded to the house to apprehend her. She had only time to hide behind a

MALAGASY CHRISTIANS READING THE SCRIPTURES SECRETLY.

mat before the soldiers entered and demanded that she should be given up. She listened to every word, fearful that her breathing should betray her. After a time the master of the house went out and the soldiers went with him to watch his movements. At once she made her escape by another way. On several other occasions she was in similar danger, and her life was preserved as by a miracle.

At last they heard that the Rev. D. Johns had ventured to Tamatave from Mauritius in order to find out the circumstances of the churches, and, if possible, to render them help and counsel. Two of the fugitives set off to see him, and he gladly agreed to try to arrange their escape from the island. On receiving the intelligence, Rafaravavy and four friends, with two faithful servants, set out for the coast. They travelled four days and nights without entering a house, suffering much from exposure and hunger, but more from anxiety lest they should be discovered. When they came within sight of Tamatave they hid themselves in the jungle, sending one of the servants with a note to a Christian friend. The servant returned with the news that all was well, and that at nightfall their friend would come in a canoe to convey them to his dwelling. This friend was an officer in the army and also a local judge. He came according to his message, and shortly the exhausted fugitives were under a friendly roof, partaking of refreshment and uniting in praise to God.

Shortly after, a ship arrived from Mauritius. They cut their hair and dressed in sailor's clothes; a friend went to the quay to divert the attention of the guards, and meanwhile they crept to the water's edge, got into a boat, pushed off from the land, rowed over the shimmering waters of the bay, and then climbed on the deck of the vessel, which was anchored off shore. The overpowering emotions of the Christians could find no expression for a time, and then, when self-possession returned, they asked leave to sing a hymn of praise. Permission was given, and the captain and crew gathered round to listen as the sweet song rose from their lips.

They reached Mauritius on the 14th of October, 1838. In a month's time they were joined by the generous judge and his nephew, who had entertained them in Tamatave and aided their escape. The part they had taken in the matter had been discovered and reported to the Government, and they had to fly for their lives.

The rescued Christians after resting a while in Mauritius sailed for England, arriving early in May, 1839, and being warmly welcomed by the Directors of the London Missionary Society. They remained nearly three years in this country, becoming acquainted with many friends, all of them, but Rafaravavy especially, making a good impression by their intelligence, their meekness and evident sincerity.

They returned to Mauritius in 1842. A piece of ground was obtained and a house built at Moka, in which Rafaravavy resided till her death, gathering round her the fugitives who kept coming from Madagascar, providing them with a comfortable refuge until they could be otherwise provided for, and encouraging them to continued hope and trust in Christ. After her death the house was still kept as a mission centre, and Simeon, the last survivor of the fugitives, laboured earnestly as a missionary among his own countrymen until he also passed away.

The third victim of the fierce persecution was Ravahiny, a beautiful young lady who had been divorced by her husband because she had become a Christian. Her father denied her a shelter, and all her relatives combined to accomplish her death. She was forced to drink the tangena water, and perished under its effects. Then three females were accused of associating for Christian worship. When the soldiers visited their house to arrest them, two of the three were reading the Bible. One of them escaped, and the other was beaten by the soldiers. Her Bible fell from her dress while she was being punished. She was dragged to the house of the officer, and six men beat her savagely to induce her to reveal the names of her friends. This she steadfastly refused to do. The next day she was taken before the chief officer, and when she again refused to give the desired information was sentenced to be flogged until she did so. After being beaten she swooned with the torture and loss of blood. She was sold into slavery and ordered to drink the tangena water, but escaped before this ordeal was administered, and was not heard of again.

The queen, whose thirst for blood seemed to wax more fierce, now commanded that the soldiers were to bind, hands and feet, any Christians they arrested, dig a pit and cast them therein and pour upon them boiling water until they died. They were then to fill up the pit and proceed with their cruel work. This was commanded under the pretence that so many Christians could not have escaped had they not possessed some charm which might injure others, and which made it unsafe for them to be brought to the capital for trial.

In May, 1840, sixteen Christians, some who had been imprisoned, and others who had been forced to drink the tangena water but had survived, commenced a journey to the coast, intending to escape from the island. The company contained Paul, the old diviner, and Joshua, one of the most pious and devoted of the native pastors. Mr. Griffiths now resided at the capital as a trader, and a Dr. Powell from Mauritius had also recently settled there. These gentlemen very generously assisted the party in starting on their journey. But they were betrayed, and five weeks after their flight they all again entered the capital as prisoners, save one, a young woman, who had miraculously escaped. They were dragged before the judges, and each of them questioned separately as to the names of other Christians. They refused to give them, so they were remanded awaiting the pleasure of the queen concerning them.

One young man and a young woman were confined in the same house. During the night while the guard slept the young man gnawed the cords asunder which bound his wrist, and then untied those at his feet. He went to release his fellow prisoner, but found the soldier in charge lying asleep on the cords which bound her. He escaped through the window of his prison, and lived to testify in after years to the sufferings of the martyrs. Mr. Jones, the first missionary to Madagascar, was in the capital at the time, and sought to comfort the minds of the captives.

On the morning of July 9, the people were summoned to the palace by the firing of cannon. An immense number assembled, and the royal decision as to the captives was announced. Eleven were condemned to be executed, but of these two had escaped. The remaining nine were ordered to be taken and exhibited before Mr. Griffith's house, then to be conveyed to a rugged hill, nearly opposite the palace, and put to death. The captives were too weak to walk, so they were tied to poles and carried to the house of their former pastor; but all were calm, and engaged in prayer. Serenity and joy were on all their countenances. One young woman testified of Christ to the guards and executioners as they carried her along.

When the fatal spot was reached they all assumed the attitude of prayer, and were at once speared. The heads of Paul and Joshua were struck off and elevated on poles as a warning to the people not to forsake the idols of the land. The queen sent word that for aiding the escape of the offenders Mr. Griffiths must pay fines amounting to about thirty pounds. He was also commanded to leave Antananarivo in a fortnight, and to return at his peril. He was in great danger for the short time he remained, and finally left Madagascar on the 1st of September, 1840.

The next to gain a martyr's crown were two Christians who had gone amongst the Sakalàvas in order to draw them into the fold of Christ. On returning sometime afterwards to the capital, they were arrested and tortured in order to induce them to betray their associates. When they were put on their trial, they declared that they had gone voluntarily to the Sakalàvas to teach them the Word of God, that thereby these people might be led to give up their habits of plunder and violence, and lead good and happy lives. Sentence of death was passed upon them, and they were sent to their native place to undergo their execution. They met their end with great fortitude and joy, exclaiming to their fellow-believers: "Farewell, beloved friends, God will cause us this day to meet with Him in paradise." After being speared, their heads were struck off and set on poles in a public place as a warning to the people.

A more cruel outrage still was perpetrated in about three months after the deaths of these men. One morning a paper was found fastened on the wall of a house in Antananarivo. It was a leaf from St. Matthew's Gospel with the words underlined: "Woe unto you scribes and pharisees, hypocrites, for ye shut up the kingdom of heaven against men, for ye neither go in yourselves, neither suffer ye them that are entering to go in." The queen was told of the occurrence, and she sent forth an announcement that the person guilty of the act must accuse himself within four days, or if he were afterwards found out, he should be cut into pieces as small as bullets. No one answered the summons, and at the end of the period named, Raharo, one of the head teachers in the Government schools and a number of others, were arrested. Raharo was forced to undergo the tangena ordeal, and died from its effects. Two others of those arrested were executed, and their bodies chopped as fine as mincemeat and burned. No evidence was offered to prove that any of these had committed the offence which had so enraged Ranavalona. They were reputed to be Christians, and they could read and write. This was quite sufficient transgression in the eyes of their accusers.

In 1843 the Mission lost one of its most valuable friends in the death of Rev. David Johns. He had been engaged in the work of promoting the evangelisation of the natives for about eighteen years. Although he had been expelled by the queen two years before his death, he had made several voyages between Madagascar and Mauritius, trying with all his power to sustain the faith of the persecuted flock, helping the fugitives to make their escape from the unfriendly shore, and providing them with shelter when they needed it. He had been of signal service to the Mission in its best days as a preacher and pastor, and had also written several hymns in the native language, which are still being sung in the public services; and above all he had contributed to the Christian literature of the Malagasy a translation of the Pilgrim's Progress, which tended greatly to console and cheer the Christians in their afflictions. He was a man of loving and gentle spirit, untiring in his enthusiasm for the great work to which he had consecrated his life. He was engaged in endeavouring to aid the escape of some Christian fugitives to the island of Nòsy Bè when he was struck down by fever and died at the age of fifty, a martyr to the cause he loved so well. An appropriate monument was erected to his memory at Nòsy Bè by Sir John Marshall, commander of H.M.S. *Isis*.

During the persecution, which lasted from 1839 to 1843, the Christians were not without their encouragements and consolations. The splendid testimony borne by the martyrs of the sufficiency of Divine Grace to sustain them in the darkest hour, deeply impressed the hearts of the spectators who gathered at the executions, and even of the soldiers who carried out the fatal sentence. There were continual though secret accessions to the Church, and to the honour of the members be it recorded that they faithfully stood by each other under the severest strain, and that no cruelty or torture could force them to betray their fellows. Thus the wrath of man was turned to the praise of Him in whose hand are the hearts of men.

CHAPTER V.

THE FIRE OF SUCCESSIVE PERSECUTIONS.

"Not first the bright and after that the dark,
But first the dark and after that the bright;
First the thick cloud and then the rainbow's arc,
First the dark grave, then resurrection light."—*Bonar.*

THERE was a lull in the cruel persecution of the Christians of Madagascar from 1843 to 1849. Very difficult and threatening disputes arose between the queen and both France and England, which fully engaged the attention of the Government. This period of respite was of very great advantage to the Christians, and while it lasted, the Gospel spread rapidly. Help came also from a most unexpected quarter. A military officer who was frequently engaged at the palace, in his journeys to and fro, sometimes took with him his nephew, who was a Christian. An acquaintance sprang up between this young man and the son of Ranavalona, the heir-apparent to the throne, then sixteen years of age. In the intercourse which ensued, the Christian religion became a frequent topic of conversation between these two, and Rakatond-radama, or Radama the young, became deeply interested in the subject. He was of a kind and gentle spirit—as complete a contrast as could be to his ferocious mother.

About this time a young man named Ramaka, or, as he afterwards was called, Rasalasala, "the bold one," rose up as a mighty preacher of the Gospel. He had been converted and baptised years before, and now, when the Church was deprived of its foreign pastors, the Spirit of God came upon him in great power, and he boldly preached to large assemblies of his countrymen. The young prince was led by his friend to go and listen to this man. He was greatly impressed, and went to hear the preacher repeatedly. Then he invited some of the Christians to his own house to instruct him in the Scriptures and pray with him. He was deeply moved with the wrongs and sufferings of the followers of Christ, and he felt constrained to befriend them in every possible way. Prince Rakatond had a cousin, called Prince Ramonja, the son of his mother's eldest sister. He was older than Rakatond, but very similar in disposition, and was regarded with much favour by the queen. He also was led to attend the meetings of the Christians, and became a convert to their teaching. He joined his young cousin in his friendship towards them, and opened his house for worship.

The nephew of the Prime Minister joined the Church also, so that as it was in the days of St. Paul, so now there were to be found, even in the days of trial, saints in "Cæsar's household." The conversion of this young man was remarkable. The prime minister sent him to the Christian meetings to obtain the names of all those present. He went and advised them at once to disperse, as mischief was being determined against them. When he was asked for the list of names he answered: "There is none." His uncle denounced him as a Christian and asserted he must lose his head. The young man at once declared himself. He said: "I am a Christian, you can put me to death, but I must pray." The uncle was overcome by his boldness and by the play of affection and replied: "No, you shall not die." The young man might be assassinated but could not be intimidated. These wonderful events no doubt contributed to keep down the persecuting spirit for a time.

In the interval the Christians were very active. Those who were hiding in the hilly districts were resorted to by many to be instructed in the things of God, and numerous converts were made. Some who were still in chains and imprisoned in their own houses were visited by many friends, and they constantly read and expounded the Scriptures, and engaged in worship in their presence. Numbers even of their guards were converted, and through their intercession the fetters on the limbs of the prisoners were relaxed and then cast off altogether. These prisoners employed much of their time in copying portions of the Bible, and in repairing torn fragments which they had been able to conceal and preserve. In the Museum of the London Missionary Society are exhibited some of these fragments. Many of them are sewn together with fibres of bark; others have strips of paper gummed along the margins, and numbers of them are stained and discoloured by having been buried in the ground, or hidden in the thatch of the roof, or the hole in the wall. In this period of respite, by the faith and devotion of the saints, the Word of the Lord grew mightily and prevailed.

A worse storm-cloud still gathered and burst upon the Malagasy Church in the early part of 1849. The queen was enraged to find that her kingdom, in spite of edicts, of bloodshed and murders, was rapidly becoming Christian. She therefore resolved to have recourse to severer measures, and to utterly exterminate the Gospel. In this determination she was encouraged by Ramboasalàma, the cousin of Rakatond, and his rival claimant to the throne. In February a popular assembly was held, and in a royal message Ranavalona demanded to know why her subjects had not given up praying, in view of her commands and the penalties which had been denounced against any who forsook the idols of the country. The Christians firmly but respectfully answered that they could not give up praying—that their prayers brought not ill but good to the queen and her kingdom and to themselves.

The storm broke by two houses belonging to Prince Ramonja, which had been used as gathering places by the Christians, being demolished, and all the materials carried away by the wreckers. In a week an order was issued that all Christians should accuse themselves in their own districts. The opportunity for self-accusation was afforded that a lighter punishment than death might be inflicted on the less guilty ones. The commissioners in each district sought to persuade the people to take an oath recognising the idols and invoking curses on themselves if they abandoned them, but they were confronted everywhere by a bold and noble firmness on the part of the persecuted. At Vonizongo, a woman stood forth before the judge, and said: "I do not pray to wood and stones, nor to the mountains. I pray to God alone, for He is great." The officers cried: "Wretch! will you not pray to the spirits of your ancestors and to the idols?" She answered: "I cannot pray to these; it is God alone that I serve." Another Christian testified in like words, adding: "For He alone is worthy to receive honour and praise."

A nobleman, descended from a former king, when brought before the judges witnessed for God so boldly that they advised that public examinations of the offender should cease, as his heroism drew forth much admiration from the bystanders. This man, Rainitraho by name, was burnt to death, and amidst the flames bore clear testimony for Jesus. At a place called Analakely, a Christian was asked to take the oath to the idols, and replied: "I shall not pray to wood and stone. Steps are made of stone, and houses are made of wood, and the idols are only cuttings of wood. Why should I worship them? Unto God alone should men offer prayer and worship." One of the accused women on being examined very strongly maintained her profession, and said: "As to swearing by the queen or by one's father or brother, a lie is a lie still, whether you swear it or not. I believe in God and put my trust in Jesus Christ, the Saviour and Redeemer of all that believe in Him." This woman, with a number of others, was reserved in irons to ascertain the queen's decision as to her fate.

A young lady named Ranivo, a special favourite with Ranavalona, and who was widely respected, underwent a rigid examination by the judges. She said: "I cannot serve the idols. God only will I serve while life shall last, for He has given me life and spirit, a higher spiritual life to worship Him, and for that reason I will worship Him alone." The officer replied: "Perhaps you are ill, or suffering from some charm, or deranged in your mind; consider well lest the queen condemn you, and you suffer to no purpose." She answered: "I am not deranged, nor am I ill; God has given me a spirit to worship Him, and I should be filled with dread were I to cease to pray unto Him." Then the order came, "Bind her."

So also many others bore similar brave testimony and the captives were remanded till the morrow, being pronounced by the officers, "stubborn and obstinate people." They were heavily ironed and put in prison until their punishment was fixed.

The Christians who were still free met at midnight and remained in fervent prayer until at break of day the booming of cannon and the rolls of musketry summoned the people in multitudes to hear the royal message. The prisoners, eighteen in number, were brought forth and were ranged on the plain in groups, according to the measure of their supposed guilt. They presented a pitiable sight,

> "Not as the conqueror comes,
> They the true hearted came."

Each man and woman was tied by cords to two poles; they were wrapped in coarse, ragged and dirty matting, rags being thrust into their mouths to prevent them witnessing for Christ. Yet those eighteen were conquerors of the truest kind. Brave John Lambert, the English martyr, said as he was being led to the stake: "Crowns are distributed to-day, and I go to receive mine." This saintly group would soon be triumphant over human malice and persecuting rage; the sharpness of death would quickly bring to them "glory, honour, immortality and eternal life."

Bands of music, regiments of soldiers, flags and standards all gave pomp and importance to the occasion, and amidst solemn silence the decision of the queen was announced. Four of the prisoners who belonged to the nobility, two being husband and wife, were condemned to be consumed by fire; the remaining fourteen were to be hurled from a lofty rock at Ampamarinana, to the west of the palace, and their families sold into perpetual slavery.

In addition to these eighteen, one hundred and seventeen were consigned to hard labour and chains for life, with public flogging added for one hundred and five of them. Sixty-four were fined heavily, indeed ruinously, while lighter fines were imposed on sixteen hundred and forty-three who were guilty of simply *attending* public worship. All the officers of the army or in the civil service who were involved in the charges were deprived of office or degraded in rank. It is supposed that nearly three thousand were affected by these sentences. Prince Ramonja was among those thus degraded. The prince royal was accused of attending Divine worship, but the queen was a mother in feeling and she saved him from any persecution, saying: "Rakatond is young; he does not know what is proper and he is my only son."

When the sentences were all pronounced a terrific noise was kept up by beating drums, large and small, to terrify the prisoners. But they failed in their object.

The Christians were quite calm. The gags had been removed from their mouths and they sang a hymn concerning the heavenly land they were so soon to enter. The four nobles were conveyed to the top of a high hill called Faravohitra. As they were taken they sang the hymn, "Going home to God," and so refuted the prediction of one of their persecutors that when death came they would be as much afraid of it as others.

When the selected place was reached a large pile of wood was put up and they were fastened to stakes. The fire was kindled, and as the flames rose round them they lifted up their voices in songs of praise, shouting in their ecstasy, "Lord Jesus, receive our spirits." "Lay not this sin to their charge." "His name, His praise, shall endure for ever and ever." Showers of rain came and put out the flames. The fires were rekindled more than once, and while the sufferers waited for their summons a glorious threefold rainbow arched the heavens, one end resting on the spot where the martyrs stood. The spectators were appalled at the sight, and fled in terror, believing it to be a sign of heaven's favour to the dying ones. Prayers and praises to God rose as long as a spark of life continued in the martyrs, and then they gently departed to the world where "there is no more pain."

The fourteen condemned ones who now remained were led to the top of "The Rock of Hurling," as it has since been called. It has been often compared to the Tarpeian Rock of Rome; but no scene ever took place on that spot at all comparable in moral grandeur with what transpired on this high precipice. It forms part of the bold cliffs by which the western side of the capital descends to the plain. The narrow plat-

THE FIRE OF SUCCESSIVE PERSECUTIONS. 95

form of rock at the top is not far from the royal palace. The height, from the top to the plain below, is about 150 feet. The fourteen who were to suffer, and Ranivo, the young woman already referred to, wrapped in

"THE ROCK OF HURLING."

matting, were firmly bound with ropes and were lowered a short distance over the edge of the rock. It was expected that at this point their courage would fail and they would recant. They were asked if they would cease to pray, and each firmly answered "No."

Then the rope by which they were suspended was cut; they fell about sixty feet on a projecting ledge and rebounded and fell among broken masses of rock into the plain below. One of the brave sufferers begged, on the edge of the rock, to be allowed to breathe a short prayer. His request was granted and he prayed aloud fervently; then he rose from his knees and addressed the people with great power, until they were amazed, and many of them overcome with awe. Then he was hurled over the edge and was heard singing as his body fell down the steep decline.

By order of the queen, Ranivo was stationed where she could see her friends fall. She was then asked whether she would worship the idols and save her life. She refused, and begged that she might go with her friends to heaven. An officer struck her on the head, saying: "You are a fool; you are mad." A message was sent to the queen that she was insane, and should be put in safe keeping.

The bodies of the sufferers were gathered up, and dragged to the spot where the nobles had been burnt; a great fire was kindled, and the remains were cast into the flames. The lurid glare was watched from the windows of the palace, and by multitudes of bystanders, who were intended to be intimidated by the weird sight. This day—the 28th of March, 1849—was the most glorious one which ever dawned in Madagascar; the crowds assembled were deeply impressed. The cruelty of the persecutors was defeating its own purpose; the natives were becoming convinced that there was a power in Christianity to uphold the heart of man in the severest trial and torture, and many of them declared that it must be Divine.

So the Word of the Lord had free course, and was glorified; converts were gathered, believers were multiplied, and in the capital seven secret meetings for worship were held, and sixty-eight members in one church alone celebrated regularly each month the Supper of the Lord.

Prince Ramonja was treated with great hardship. He was reduced to the rank of a common soldier, and allowed only the scantiest clothing. His attached friend Prince Rakatond tried to comfort him, visiting him frequently, weeping with him, and sending him food from his own house. The health of Ramonja suffered severely, and he was an invalid for the rest of his life, but he ever remained a firm friend and a prudent counsellor of the followers of Jesus.

A large number of the other Christians who had been fined were sent as convicts to work in the quarries of Mantasoa, where a large building was in course of erection. They were kept in the poorest way, and their tasks made cruelly heavy. When the work of building was finished, they were made to drag heavy logs and beams of timber from the forest. Thus they were punished till 1852 when Prince Ramboasalàma and the chief persecutors proposed to sentence them for a longer term to the same drudgery. But the prince royal and others pleaded for them and they were released. A new commander-in-chief who had been appointed boldly addressed the queen on their behalf, and said: "They have suffered twice the punishment to which they were sentenced, why should they be sentenced again? The thunderbolt never strikes twice."

After his release Prince Ramonja became an officer in the palace. He attended the meetings of the

Christians, and even spoke to the queen and the members of the royal family about the Gospel. The queen's affection for her sister, the mother of Ramonja, was his protection against a new prosecution. The emissaries of the Government kept up an unremitting search for any who continued to read the Bible or meet together for prayer. Prince Rakatond and his cousin sought to shelter and befriend the poor believers, who were being harried; they supplied them freely with money for their needs, and on one occasion Rakatond went to a place where a number of them were in confinement and loosed their bonds, telling their keeper to say, if he were called to account for them, that he had released them. The secret meetings for prayer in the city were sometimes attended by those who had been condemned to wear irons for life, and it was a pathetic sight to see them, with a fetter round the neck and chains fastened from it to the wrists, and with a fetter round the waist and chains from it to the feet, struggling along under the great weight. The believers throughout the country were numbered by thousands and were continually receiving additions.

The partial respite from persecution from 1852 to the last and greatest trial the Church of Madagascar was subjected to was occasioned partly by the death of Rainiharo, the prime minister, who had largely incited the queen in her conduct, and who had been the bitterest of all the enemies of the Christians. He was succeeded by his son, who was an intimate friend of the young prince royal, and who did not inherit the persecuting spirit of his father. Prince Rakatond became secretary of state, and an officer of the palace.

His duty it was to publish the royal edicts, and it was rumoured that his mother was desirous of abdicating in his favour. In consequence of these changes there was a palpable alteration for the better in the treatment of the Christians. The London Missionary

REV. WILLIAM ELLIS.

Society encouraged by these favourable tidings felt that it might safely send a commissioner to visit the island, for the purposes of investigation and of strengthening the hands of the Christians. The Rev. William Ellis was intrusted with the important work. No more suitable man could have been appointed. He began his missionary life in 1816, accompanying the well-known Rev. John Williams to the South Sea Islands, where he spent some years of faithful service, and then became foreign secretary to the Society. He had gathered up an immense quantity of information about the island of Madagascar, and of course knew intimately everything about the Mission. He had published "The History of Madagascar," in two volumes, which is the most full and correct account yet supplied of the country, and from which all subsequent writers on the subject have drawn much of their information.

Mr. Ellis was therefore well prepared beforehand for the mission to which he was appointed. He was accompanied by Mr. Cameron, and they arrived at Tamatave in July, 1853. They had a cordial reception from the officers of that port and Mr. Ellis forwarded a letter to the queen seeking permission to come up to the capital. In three weeks a reply was received to the effect that the Government was so engaged with pressing business that he could not be received, and advising his return lest he should become a victim of the island fever. This was a polite notice to quit, but in the meantime Mr. Ellis had gathered much information as to the condition of the churches. He received a letter from Prince Ramonja, asking for copies of the Bible, stating also that he held regular meetings for worship in his apartments in the court of the palace, and that the band played at the same time in order that they might not be heard by the queen or her emissaries.

In June of 1854 Mr. Ellis made another trip from Mauritius to Tamatave, and again sought leave to

MODE OF TRAVELLING IN MADAGASCAR.

visit Antananarivo. But the cholera was raging fiercely at Mauritius, and the Malagasy Government was justly alarmed concerning this awful disease. He was not permitted to proceed farther than the coast, but during the few weeks he lingered there he had almost daily intercourse with Christians, who came from all the districts around to visit him and have spiritual intercourse. He took down full accounts of the bloody trials to which the Church had been subjected during the years of persecution, and he conversed with many who had suffered fines and imprisonment for their attachment to their beliefs. The officers who had been forced to labour in the quarries and forests of Mantasoa showed him the wounds and bruises, "marks of the Lord Jesus," which they had received while engaged in their terrible slavery.

The great want of the churches was copies of the Bible. The officers at Tamatave had orders to seize all books which were brought into the country. Mr. Ellis, in going to and from his vessel and the shore, used to conceal about his person as many copies as he could. When his boat touched the beach he had to leap from its bow to the land, with several custom-house officers standing around, and he trembled lest a volume should be jerked to the ground, and very thankful he was when he could get to his lodging and unload his treasures in safety. In this way he was able during successive visits to distribute 1500 Bibles, Testaments, and Psalms to the people who hungered for the Word of God.

Having done what he could, Mr. Ellis left Madagascar in September, and after visiting the stations of the South African Mission, arrived safely in London.

After leaving the island, Mr. Ellis received a letter from the Government stating that as the cholera had ceased at Mauritius, all objection to him visiting Antananarivo was removed. Therefore he paid a third visit to Madagascar, arriving at Tamatave in July, and at the capital in August, 1856.

At this time there was no active persecution being carried out, but the profession and practice of the Christian religion was still forbidden, and every fortnight the royal command that strict search was to be made for those who gathered for worship, or were in the habit of praying to God, was read out in the hearing of the people. Therefore Mr. Ellis was obliged to use the utmost caution in his intercourse with the native members. At the instigation of Prince Ramboasalàma, a vigilant watch was kept, and the names recorded of all Christians who were seen to visit him. He took every opportunity of encouraging the hearts of the faithful, and assured them of the deepest sympathy and prayers of those in England who had first sent them the Gospel. He relieved those who were in deep poverty, and scattered copies of the sacred books wherever he could do so with safety. He received every mark of outward courtesy from the queen and her officers, but there is no doubt that they were more desirous to secure the goodwill of an English visitor than to treat with politeness a missionary of the Cross. He found that it would be quite impolitic to ask for the repeal of the intolerant edicts against Christianity, and after remaining a month in the capital, he received notice to quit in the form of a civil intimation that as the rainy season was approaching it would not be well for him to prolong his visit. All that he had hoped for had not been accomplished by his visit, but good undoubtedly had been done. He had gathered much valuable information, given useful counsel, and inspired the hearts of many by helpful sympathy. He came back to England in 1857 with a store of mission news which would do much to stir the fervour and zeal of the friends of missions throughout the world.

Mr. Ellis had not left Madagascar more than about three months before there broke out a persecution as fierce and terrible as any which had gone before. It was partly induced by political events. For some years there had resided in the capital two French gentlemen, one an extensive manufacturer of glass, pottery, and other articles, and the other a large planter and merchant. They had long been utterly disgusted with the tyranny and bloodshed which had marked the reign of Ranavalona, and conceived the project of displacing her and placing Prince Rakatond upon the throne. The hope of personal advantage as well as the desire of ridding the country of a bigoted tyrant actuated them in this movement.

Mr. Lambert, the latter of these gentlemen, went to France in order to bespeak help from the Emperor, Louis Napoleon. In this he failed, and returned to Antananarivo. The plot was found out, and the queen was so enraged that she ordered the French gentlemen, with Madame Ida Pfeiffer, the celebrated traveller, who was then in the city, and also two Jesuit priests, who were there in disguise, to quit the country at once. Then she considered how she might vent her passion. Nero gratified his cruelty by fastening upon the Christians of Rome the unfounded charge of having set fire to that city, and Ranavalona fixed upon the Christians as being the natural object of her resentment now.

There was not the slightest ground for supposing that the followers of Christ had taken part in this conspiracy. Some of them *might* have heard of it, and it would not be surprising if they had secretly hoped for its success, but more than this they had not done. The queen, however, desired a victim, the laws against Christianity were still in force, the Christians were multiplying in spite of them, and therefore she resolved to make one more desperate effort to stamp them out. A villain, who had professed to be converted in order to become acquainted with those who assembled for worship, supplied a list of seventy persons whom he averred to be concerned in the conspiracy, but Prince Rakatond got hold of it and tore it to pieces. The Christians were warned of the storm which was about to rage around them, and fled in large companies to distant parts of the island.

An assembly of the people was called by the firing of cannon on the 3rd of July, when it was announced that the queen had heard that in and around the city there were many Christians. These were ordered to report themselves within fifteen days on pain of death. Only a few obeyed the summons. Bands of soldiers went in search of fugitives, but few were captured. Efforts were renewed repeatedly to apprehend them, and rewards were freely offered for their discovery. The queen declared that she would search to the bowels of the earth and to the bottom of lakes and rivers to find them. At length about 300 were arrested and presented for trial. Six of them were discovered hidden in a pit and covered with straw. The soldiers had searched for them in vain, and were leaving the place when one heard a faint cough, and so the search was renewed and the helpless ones found. They were bound and marched to the capital, and with them the inhabitants of the village who had befriended them.

Prince Ramonja and the commander-in-chief laboured strenuously to restrain the tide of cruelty and to alleviate the sufferings of the afflicted. The prince royal also saved many lives, and exerted himself so much in behalf of the prisoners, that, but for the love Ranavalona had for him, he would himself have been apprehended and punished. The charge which was brought against the Christians was not that of having aided in a conspiracy, but of praying, reading the Bible, and singing hymns. There was no attempt to deny the truth of these charges, nor any shrinking from the consequences of them.

More than 200 were condemned to various punishments. Those who were most signalised by their usefulness, piety, and ability, were to bear testimony for Christ by suffering death for His sake. A new punishment in Madagascar was devised to make their end more terrible, so as to operate as a deterrent on the minds of others. Fourteen were stoned on one day at Fiadana, about a mile from Ambohipotsy, and others endured the same punishment on other days. After being stoned, their heads were severed from their bodies and fixed on poles. But in the darkness of the night attached friends stole quietly to the spot, drove away the hungry dogs which had congregated for a welcome meal, and gathering up the mangled fragments of their beloved ones carried them off, that with Christian rites they might be laid in the silent grave.

Fifty-seven or more were chained together by the neck with heavy irons and driven to distant parts of the island where more than half died in their chains after enduring indescribable torture. A set of irons worn by one of these Christians is in the museum of the London Missionary Society, and weighs fifty-six pounds. Fifty took the tangena water, eight of whom died, and others experienced permanent injury from the ordeal. If any of those who were chained together died, their comrades had to drag the dead bodies about with them until they also died from the contamination, thus reviving in this other form the horrors of the early Christian martyrdoms. Some were taken to the "Rock of Hurling," and there bravely suffered death for their Master. Many others were sent into slavery and only redeemed by ruinous sacrifices on the part of their friends, whilst a few who had received sentence of death escaped and remained in hiding for years, often suffering privations which were almost worse than death itself.

This awful persecution was the worst which had been experienced by the Church in respect of the large number of prominent members who were cut off by it, but it was the last convulsive effort of a dying heathenism to assert its power against the sovreignty of the Lord Jesus. There was, in the year 1860, an attempt made to raise the spirit of persecution once more, but the effort recoiled upon the head of the party who promoted it. Thus the *remainder* of wrath was restrained by the power of God, and after about eighteen years of intolerance, bloodshed and murder,

THE FIRE OF SUCCESSIVE PERSECUTIONS.

the persecutors had to confess with Julian, the apostate Emperor of Rome: "Galilean, Thou hast conquered!" The end of the persecution left the Christians more pure and devoted, more united to each other and attached to Jesus than when it began, and, marvellous to relate, the blood of the martyrs had become the seed of the Church, and the number of believers had steadily increased as the fiery trial had passed upon them.

CHAPTER VI.

THE DAWN OF FREEDOM AND PROSPERITY.

> "Let thy gold be cast in the furnace,
> Thy red gold precious and bright;
> Do not fear the hungry fire,
> With its caverns of burning light;
> And thy gold shall return more precious,
> Free from every spot and stain;
> For gold must be tried by fire,
> As a heart must be tried by pain."—*A. A. Procter.*

AFTER the last persecution had spent its force the Christian Church in Madagascar held on its perilous way, being still subject to pains and penalties. Many of its members were kept in prison, or were bound in chains, or hiding in mountains, dens, or caves of the earth. Numbers of them must have suffered severe privations but for the generous help of the Princes Rakatond and Ramonja, who exhausted all their means to supply them with food, clothes and money.

But relief was at hand. After a long dark night the sky was flecked with indications of dawn. Early in 1861 the queen's health showed evident signs of decline. So long as she was able to attend to public business her agents, headed by Prince Ramboasalàma, were eager to enforce the laws in operation against the Christians, and her spirit waxed more cruel towards the people generally. As she became weaker, the treatment of the Christians was milder, some of the sentences passed upon them were partially relaxed, and of those sold into permanent slavery many were allowed to be redeemed.

The public mind became anxious concerning impending changes. Portents in the sky and on the island were said to have been observed, indicating that a decisive event was about to occur. The queen, probably feeling that her end was approaching, gave herself to much prayer to her idols. She sought change of air, she tried charms and took medicine, but all in vain, she wasted still. Prince Rakatond, his wife and all the members of the royal family were ordered to remain in the palace, and the soldiers on guard were increased to five hundred, so as to be in readiness for any emergency.

On the 16th of July Ranavalona died. She was scarcely regretted by anyone, although a fortnight was spent in funeral ceremonies. Then her remains were carried with solemn pomp through crowds of spectators to her sepulchre. Orders were given as usual that the people must shave their heads, put on sombre clothing, and discontinue their amusements. But there was scarcely any real sorrow manifested. Thirty-three years she had exercised a harsh and bigoted rule over her unhappy subjects. For twenty-five years she had carried out a spirit of cruel intolerance towards the Christians, and had earned for herself the title of "the bloody Mary" of modern days. Her death was, therefore, welcomed by the whole nation as a relief from a nightmare which had long rested on the moral and educational life of the people. While intending and endeavouring to extirpate Christianity from her realm she had been the means, by the overruling power of a wise Providence, of purifying, proving and winnowing the people of God, so that the Church of the future in Madagascar might be the more powerful and glorious.

Prince Rakatond had long been considered the heir-apparent to the throne, but, as before mentioned, he had a powerful and unscrupulous rival in his cousin Prince Ramboasalàma, the elder brother of Prince Ramonja. This ambitious and cruel man professed to be willing to offer allegiance to Rakatond. But he had collected all the friends and retainers he could influence, and had them under arms at the time of the queen's death, so that there was good reason to anticipate that he meditated an attempt to seize the crown. He was favoured by the prime minister and some of the leading officials, and he might have succeeded in such an attempt but for the forethought of the commander-in-chief. This able officer on the night before the queen's death placed a cordon of troops not only round the royal palace but also round the palace of Ramboasalàma. When the queen died he increased the number and strength of the guard, and gave orders that no one should be allowed to go in or pass out of the palaces. When the queen's death was announced to the people, Rakatond was at the same time proclaimed as her successor, and while the army and the populace were giving expression to

"THE BANISHED ONES JOYFULLY MINGLED WITH THEIR FAMILIES AGAIN."

their joy, the rival claimant and his friends were detained in their own houses.

In a short time, the whole of the royal family, including Ramboasalàma, attended and took the oath of allegiance to Rakatond, who ascended the throne under the title of Radama II. The joy of the people of the capital and the district at his accession was extreme. The Christians especially were overwhelmed with thankfulness. They expressed their feelings in the words of Scripture: "When the Lord turned again the captivity of Zion we were like those that dream. Then was our mouth filled with laughter and our tongue with singing."

On the very day of his proclamation Radama announced that every man was fully at liberty to follow his own religious convictions, and that whether a man were heathen, or Christian, or Mohammedan, no one was to interfere with his opinions. But all, whatever their religion, must obey the laws of the nation.

This announcement not only gave relief to the Christians, but also satisfied the heathen, who; not understanding the idea of toleration, had feared that reprisals would be attempted for all the wrongs the Christians had endured. Closely following this act of toleration, steps were taken to restore to comfort and liberty all who had been suffering disabilities in the previous reign. The banished ones were brought out of their hiding-places, and joyfully mingled with their families again. Many who were so enfeebled by the weight of heavy chains and prolonged toil that they could not travel were carried to their former homes by royal messengers, and the king restored property and land to those who had been despoiled of them for their adherence to their Christian principles.

Although the young king had never professed himself a Christian, he had long since given up all faith in the national idols. The priests of the old order, on one occasion, boasted before him of the power of the idols, and assured him that no one could harm or destroy them. The king called a number of Christians and sent them to burn down one of the idol houses, and he stood by and watched the flames as they consumed the building. This event not only decided the king as to the helplessness of idols, but also shook the faith in them of many of the young men of the capital. All idols were expelled from the royal palace, the attendance of the priests and diviners was dispensed with, and the usual royal gifts for sacrifices were discontinued. When the priests came one day to ask for a bullock in behalf of a certain idol, the king said: "If the idol wants a bullock, let him come and ask me for one."

With one fell swoop also Radama abolished the cruel tangena ordeal, with sorceries, divinations, and superstitious ceremonies. He gave opportunities for all to approach him who had complaints to make, or who desired justice to be administered, and by his wise and magnanimous treatment of the traditional enemies of his own tribe, the Sakalàvas, he attached them to him by strong ties of friendship. As a result of these wise and politic measures, the reign of Radama opened with the highest promise of usefulness, and had he taken all his steps with equal prudence his reign might have been both happy and long.

Unfortunately he did not choose his principal

advisers and helpers in the State with discretion. He dismissed nearly all the ministers of Ranavalona and even took little notice of the commander-in-chief who had been mainly instrumental in placing him on the throne. He appointed to the chief offices in the Government a number of young men of no experience or ability, but who had been friends and companions of his youth. Such statesmen were not likely to add much to the stability of the throne. In order also to increase the trade and wealth of his kingdom, Radama abolished all duties and tariffs upon imports, and the first result of this step was that the ports were inundated with intoxicating liquors. Sixty thousand gallons of rum were brought from Mauritius in a week. Houses were speedily opened for its sale in all directions, and drunkenness with its train of attendant evils rapidly spread among the people. French and English traders flocked to the capital, and as the king was of a jovial disposition, a love of indulgence in drinking and other vices took hold upon him. Those around him encouraged him in a downward course. Foreign traders, political opponents, and hypocritical flatterers, played upon his weaknesses for their various objects and incited him to his ruin.

Very soon after the death of Ranavalona, the Christians re-established Divine worship in the capital. Eleven houses were opened as meeting-places, all of them being crowded with worshippers. Then they set to work to erect chapels, and five were speedily built. They were very rude structures, with mud walls and thatched roofs, but they were filled with earnest men and women who met to rejoice that religious freedom had been restored in the land.

When the news of Radama's accession to the throne reached England, the London Missionary Society took prompt measures to occupy the field again. Rev. W. Ellis was requested to proceed at once to Antananarivo to prepare the way for new agents to settle there and to secure sites for the building of churches. In a few days he took ship and after a favourable voyage reached Mauritius. He was detained there for several weeks as the season was most unhealthy in Madagascar, but he did what was possible under the circumstances by correspondence. He learned that a number of French Romish priests had arrived, and some had penetrated to the capital, but that the Christians anxiously desired the return of their old pastors and teachers. Mr. Ellis wrote to them encouraging them to keep united and faithful, and assuring them that arrangements were being made to supply the needs of the Mission as rapidly as possible. He also wrote to the king, informing him that he was only waiting for an opportunity to come to Madagascar, and entreating him not to allow the spots consecrated by the blood of the martyrs to be sold or occupied till he arrived.

Mr. Ellis reached Tamatave in May, 1862, accompanied by several traders and a number of the Christian exiles who had taken refuge at Mauritius. A boat full of Christians came out to meet the vessel and welcome Mr. Ellis as he approached the bay. As he stepped on shore he was met by a royal messenger, who handed him a letter of welcome from the king. Christians crowded round him, affording a delightful contrast to the experience of his former visit, when he could only meet them at midnight, and in secret.

The next day a thanksgiving meeting was held in a house which the king had provided for the purpose, and sixty people were present. The following day was the Sabbath, and a hundred Christians attended the public services. Mr. Ellis, both at Tamatave and during his journey through the country, had ample evidence of the mischief which was being done by the traffic in ardent spirits. He sometimes saw the entire population of a village intoxicated before twelve o'clock in the day.

As he came near the capital he saw at Ambatomanga, a large company of men by the roadside. When he was close upon them they all rose and sang a hymn. They then informed him that they had been sent by the Christians of the capital to meet and escort him, which they did by forming around him and singing hymns as they marched along. On reaching Antananarivo he found a comfortable house had been provided for his residence. Crowds of Christians, many of whom were maimed and marked by the severity of their persecution, streamed in to welcome him. Presents of oxen, sheep, pigs, poultry, and other farm produce were poured upon him, very much of which he had to distribute to the poor, as he could not make use of all.

The day after his arrival Mr. Ellis was summoned to an audience with the king and queen. He made a statement to them of the intentions of the London Missionary Society to send a company of mission agents to resume the work which had been so long interrupted. He was also the bearer of despatches from the Governor of Mauritius, one of them being a letter from Queen Victoria, assuring the king of the continued friendship of the English Government. After this reception, Mr. Ellis was besieged with crowds of Christians who gathered up from the surrounding district to welcome him. He was deeply affected when visited by the widows and children of some of those who had been burnt, stoned, or hurled over the precipice, and who themselves had suffered severe privations in the cause of Christ.

Prince Ramonja at this time was ill, and expressed a warm desire to see Mr. Ellis. In the interview, he testified his deep gratitude at the altered condition of the Christians; his son accompanied the missionary to his house, and at a meeting held in the evening united himself with the Church. The prime minister sought a long interview with Mr. Ellis in order to question him fully as to the special objects of the missionaries and other agents who were supposed to be on the way to Madagascar. The fullest information was given and he was assured that no political purposes were entertained, but that the whole aim of the Mission would be to promote the moral and social welfare of the people.

Mr. Ellis visited the spots where the martyrs had so bravely suffered death, and on the first Sunday he spent at the capital he went to the chapel at Analakely, which had been crowded since break of day. It was seven o'clock when the missionary arrived, accompanied by Prince Ramonja's son and several young chiefs. The place was densely packed with people of all ages. When they stood up to sing, the full, joyous burst of praise was thrilling to hear. There were not less than one thousand people present at the service. Other places visited on the same day

PORT LOUIS, MAURITIUS.

were equally thronged, and the gladness manifested in the meetings was overwhelming.

After a few days' sojourn in the city Mr. Ellis was asked by some of the princes and nobles to teach their sons English, and he consented to give them instruction for two hours each day. The queen sent her adopted son and the king asked him to go to the palace daily to read English with him, and this was done till within a few days of Radama's death. The king, on the death of his mother, began to erect a good stone building to be used as a school. When it was finished he desired Mr. Ellis to hold service in it each Sunday afternoon for himself and any of his court who chose to attend.

On one occasion when the members of an embassy from England, including Dr. Ryan, Bishop of Mauritius, waited upon the king, reference was made to him having saved so many lives and having shown such kindness to the Christians. Mr. Ellis was asked to reply on behalf of the king. In presence of a crowded court the missionary responded, stating that undoubtedly the king had done much for his people and for Christianity, but, he added: "There is one thing wanted—the one thing needful—he has not become a Christian himself." The king looked very serious and said to the court: "Mr. Ellis knows what is in my heart; he knows that I desire to understand and serve God, I desire—I pray to God to enlighten my mind, to teach me what I ought to know."

The Sunday afternoon service was attended by about sixty officers, and Radama was nearly always present. The greatest decorum was observed during the proceedings and impressions were made on the minds of some, which afterwards deepened and led to true conversion. But as British and French traders increased in the capital the moral conduct of Radama deteriorated. After the service was over on Sunday afternoons, a large piano was brought in, and music, singing and dancing were introduced. These were too often followed by feasting and drinking, and the king of a growing nation would be found quite drunk. Mr. Ellis faithfully expostulated with him as to his conduct and he repeatedly promised amendment. But there were too many around the king ready to encourage him and join him in his revels for these admonitions to prevail.

On the 30th of August a contingent of helpers for the Mission reached Antananarivo, containing Rev. R. Toy and Mrs. Toy, a medical missionary and his wife, Dr. and Mrs. Davidson, a schoolmaster, Mr. Stagg, and a skilled printer, Mr. Parrett. They were cordially welcomed by the king and queen; by the members of the British Embassy; and by the Christians. They were followed a few days afterwards by Revs. R. G. Hartley, M.A., W. E. Cousins, and G. Cousins, and their wives. They brought with them a beautiful copy of the English Bible as a gift from the Bible Society, which Radama readily accepted. On the Sabbath following the arrival of this company, which was the first Sunday in the month, the Christian believers held a united communion. Eight hundred were present, and it was an affecting service. All those present had been admitted to church membership by native evangelists, and had proved the reality of their profession by their fidelity to Christ in the dark night of terror and trial.

The Bishop of Mauritius, who had accompanied the British Embassy to Madagascar, conferred much with Mr. Ellis on the best way of covering the island with a knowledge of Christ. The Bishop strongly disavowed any intention of crossing the lines of those who were in the field ; but suggested that the Church Missionary Society might properly take up work along the coast, which as yet was untouched by mission effort. To this Mr. Ellis assented, saying that the mutual understanding which had prevailed between the two Societies, that they should not interfere with each other's spheres, had hitherto worked so well that he did not fear that it would be infringed in the future, and that he had already written to England suggesting that the Church Missionary Society should take up some portions of the island. In course of time this Society established a mission on the south-east coast, and the Society for the Propagation of the Gospel one on the north-east coast. The people of Madagascar have thus been saved the unedifying spectacle of rival Christian bodies diverting them from the great foundation principles, on which there is general agreement, by controversy on matters of mere Church order and administration.

Mr. Ellis took decisive action as to the erection of churches on the places where the martyrs had been translated to the heavenly world. The king very graciously acceded to his request that they should be reserved for this purpose, and a special fund was commenced in England by the London Missionary Society to provide the money required. The noble sum of £13,000 was subscribed in a short time, and steps were taken to carry out the project, which will presently be detailed.

The king and queen were publicly crowned on the 23rd of September. A vast throng assembled to witness the ceremony. There was no recognition of the idols or the idol priests, and no charms were carried near the king's person, as had been the custom heretofore. There was a company of priests in the crowd with a number of idols, which Mr. Ellis describes as being dirty pieces of silver chain, small silver balls, pieces of coral, silver ornaments representing crocodile's teeth, with strips of scarlet cloth, and one thing which looked like a red woollen cap of liberty.

The Christian churches of the capital were now properly organised. A simple statement of principles of Church order was prepared; native pastors were appointed to preside over the churches, with boards of deacons. The missionaries explained that, while willing to be associated with the native pastors, they did not desire to control the churches, but to aid in maintaining order and purity in them, and to extend Christianity to regions beyond. Mr. W. E. Cousins was associated with two native preachers in the oversight of the church at Amparibe; Mr. Ellis was appointed to that at Ambatonakanga and Mr. Toy retained the church he had gathered in the north of the city, but which afterwards worshipped at Ambohipotsy, one of the memorial sites.

In March, 1863, the king and his ministers executed deeds, by which the memorial sites were legally conveyed to the members of the Mission. The boundaries were fixed, and workmen were employed to quarry stones for the foundations and walls of a good church at Ambohipotsy. At once every member of the congregation was at work—some removing rubbish, some levelling the ground, women and children carrying earth or stones to and fro, and all of them singing for joy as they laboured. A spacious church was built on the east side of the city, and filled to excess on the day of its consecration ; and on the first Communion Sabbath fifty-eight members observed the ordinance, and ten received baptism.

While all things seemed to be working so favourably for Christianity, they were not going so happily in regard to the king and the political welfare of the nation. Radama became the dupe of Mr. Lambert, the Frenchman already referred to, who encouraged his vices, and led him to frequent fits of drunkenness. This man, while the king was intoxicated, induced him to sign a concession of rights to him over one-third of the arable land of the kingdom ; of working all its mines ; of conducting what manufactures he pleased ; and of introducing Jesuits without any limit. All these concessions were violations of the laws of the realm.

Then Radama surrounded himself with a number of dissolute young men, who really governed the island. It was no wonder that the supporters of the old superstitions began to bestir themselves. There came floating to the capital from the country districts vague and alarming rumours as to visions and voices said to be seen and heard by many who were seized with a sickness which rendered some unconscious, and which caused others to jerk and dance in an unaccountable manner. These voices, it was said, delivered warnings as to awful calamities which were about to occur on account of the apostasy of the king and his ministers from the gods of the country.

The effect of these pretended revelations on the mind of the king was very great. His mind was no doubt much weakened by his growing indulgence in sensuality and drinking. A deep melancholy fell upon him. One day he was sitting with Mr. Ellis in his palace when a number of priests and dancing-women rushed in. The women danced madly round the room, and the priests regarded Mr. Ellis with threatening looks. The king at last mustered courage to order them out of the room. Mr. Ellis was afterwards told that the party had meant to attack him, and for nine successive nights small packets of what were thought to be death warrants or sorcerer's charms were laid at the door of his house. The king, on hearing of the danger to which he was subjected, sent a guard of soldiers to watch his house nightly.

The king's mind was becoming more weak and morbid, until it was doubtful whether it had not entirely given way. It was said that he had been constrained to favour a new persecution of the Christians, but the truth of this was never proved. But he did, at the suggestion of evil advisers, proclaim that all differences of opinion, whether between individuals or villages or towns might be settled by open battle between the parties, and that the successful party should not be called to account for any that might be slain in the conflict. The wiser of the nobles stoutly opposed this decree; they went before the king on their knees and besought him to withdraw it, and to give up his evil counsellors. They pleaded in vain, however, for he refused to listen to them. As the decree was an open incitement to civil war and internal discord, the wiser statesmen of the country felt a time for action had arrived.

One day Mr. Ellis saw the plain in front of the palace covered with armed men, and was told that thirteen of the king's favourites had been seized, some of them put to death, and the remainder held in confinement. A fresh slaughter of officers and nobles followed the next day, and the day after that, being the 12th of May, 1863, the conspirators forced an entrance into the king's bedroom, and removing the queen from the scene, strangled him. As they put a cord round his neck, he said: "I have never shed blood." A mantle was cast over his head and the cord tightened, and he sank lifeless on the floor. He was murdered by the very party which had exalted him to the throne, and which had been so disappointed in the results of his reign.

There can be no doubt but that this young man had accomplished much good for his country, which was not all neutralised by the weak and wavering conduct of the last few months of his life. He had abolished religious persecution and established liberty of conscience; he had pacified the traditional enemies of his race and brought them into friendly alliance with his own tribe. He had also given new impulses to the growth of civilisation throughout his province. But he hesitated to embrace Christianity, which would have saved him from the errors and sins of his life; he associated himself with those who were not fit to be his advisers, and trusted in flatterers and boon companions, who played upon his frailties for their own profit. So what otherwise might have been a bright and prosperous reign, was thus brought to an abrupt end.

The conquering party in the palace after killing the king, had an interview with the queen, and offered her the crown upon certain conditions, which she accepted. Then was laid the foundation of a constitutional government in the island. She engaged that the sovereign should not alone have the power of sentencing any one to death or of enacting any law, but that certain representatives of the nobles and of the people along with the sovereign should have the power of life or death, and of making or altering the laws of the nation. Perfect religious freedom was also to be continued to all classes of the kingdom.

About noon the firing of cannon summoned an assembly of the people. It was then announced that the king had died during the night by his own hand, that his widow Rasoherina had succeeded to the crown, and that she had agreed to govern the kingdom on the terms already specified. Thus happily the State passed through a crisis which might have resulted in moral disaster of the worst kind. The queen was not a Christian, but a patron of the heathen party and of the idols, but at her first reception of the missionaries she assured them that they should be sustained in their liberty to worship and preach as before, and that she cordially approved of the objects they had in view.

The startling change in the crown came on the Christians with bewildering surprise. But the experience was not all unwholesome. The transition from

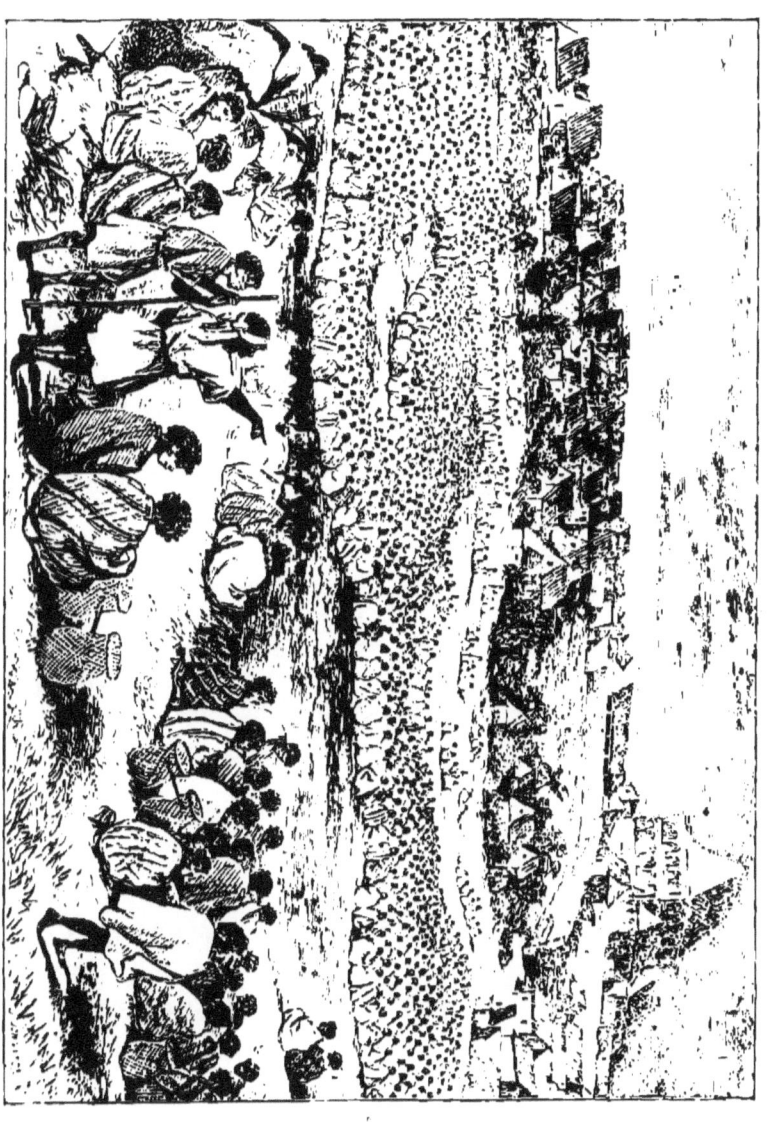

GREAT MEETING OF MALAGASY CHRISTIANS. [p. 134.

trial and persecution to prosperity and royal favour had been so sudden that many in the Church were in danger of being carried away by it. It was soon found also, that to be a Christian was no longer a reproach but rather a road to honour, and so unworthy men began to creep into the Church. This reverse came as a check upon such tendencies; it led the Christians to be more watchful, and convinced them of the instability of worldly things.

The new queen, Rasoherina, proved herself to be a good ruler. She had no partiality towards Christianity, but was, as stated, a devoted follower of the old superstitions. She was shrewd and firm in her administration, kind and merciful in her disposition, and she honourably carried out the condition on which she assumed the crown—of maintaining liberty of conscience for all her subjects. Only one thing the Christians had to complain of, viz., that many of them who were officers and work-people under the Government were obliged to work on the Sabbath day, and also to be present and take part in amusements of which they did not approve. This did not arise from unfriendliness to the Christians, but from the fact that the Government ignored the right of any one to be exempt from duty who was in its employment.

When the queen and her court were at Ambohimanga, it was several times arranged for the Christians to attend service once during the Sabbath. The queen said to them on one occasion: "I know that many of you are praying people and like to attend worship. Perhaps you are afraid that as I do not pray I shall be displeased with you for doing so. Do not think so; those who like shall go. But remember that I shall expect you who are Christians, and thus *profess* to be better than others, will *act* better than other people. I shall expect that you will not lie, or cheat, or steal, or do evil as others do, but show by your conduct what a good thing praying really is." This was an unconscious but a splendid testimony to the purity and superiority of life which the Gospel inculcates.

Mr. Ellis and his friends sought to revive the work of Christianity in the numerous villages of the district round the capital which had felt severely the strain of persecution. Mr. Toy gave much attention to the villages in the south, and gathered a group of young men whom he sought to train as preachers and pastors. Mr. W. E. Cousins did the same for the villages to the north, and in order to arouse the aggressive spirit in the heart of the churches it was resolved to hold a missionary prayer meeting of all the churches once each month. The first of these meetings was held at Analakely. Long before the appointed time crowds of people assembled, and the service had to be held in the open air in order that all might partake in it. At least 3000 were present, and it continued several hours.

Very delightful testimonies as to the growth of Christianity were constantly being reported. In one village north of the capital, the whole of the people had been ardent worshippers of the idols kept among them, but the idols were forsaken, the people took a house and set it apart for the worship of Christ. When the queen was told of this, she replied: "If any villagers are Christians and wish to discontinue idol worship they may do so; it is no offence."

DR. DAVIDSON'S HOUSE AND MEDICAL MISSION.

A medical dispensary under the management of Dr. Davidson, was now in full operation, and multitudes thronged to him daily to submit themselves to his healing art, all of whom had the opportunity also of becoming acquainted with "the Great Healer." Additional helpers had been sent out by the Society in Mr. and Mrs. Pearse and Mr. Kessler, several new churches had been built, or were in the course of erection, and a large central school had been recently opened. Mr. Stagg, the schoolmaster, was delighted with the intelligence of the Malagasy children, and declared they were capable of receiving as high an education as English children. He laboured assiduously to establish a system of education resembling in its general features that commenced by Mr. Joseph Lancaster in England. But in the midst of his useful work his life was terminated in February, 1864, seventeen months after his landing in the island.

Mr. Parrett issued from the press an immense supply of literature. A large new edition of the Bible revised by Mr. Griffiths was circulated, translations of some of the most useful religious books were prepared, as were spelling-books and other educational works. A periodical called *Good Words* was commenced on the 1st of January, 1866, and a commentary on the New Testament was in progress. Thus, in this land so recently benighted, a really Christian literature was rapidly being created.

CHAPTER VII.

A CHRISTIAN KINGDOM ESTABLISHED.

"He that goeth forth with weeping,
Bearing precious seed in love,
Never tiring, never sleeping,
Findeth mercy from above:
Soft descend the dews of heaven,
Bright the rays celestial shine,
Precious fruit will thus be given,
Through an influence all divine."—*Hastings.*

IT is time to give some account of the progress made in the erection of the churches intended to memorialise the faith and steadfastness of the Malagasy martyrs. Mr. James Sibree was invited to go out to Madagascar as architect of the proposed churches. He accepted the appointment, and leaving England arrived at Antananarivo in October, 1863. It was decided that the first site built upon should be that at Ambatonakanga, and immediate preparations were made. The first stone was laid on the 19th of January, 1864, by the prime minister, in the presence of some of the leading members of the Government and a large number of

Christians. Slowly the building progressed, and it was not till March, 1866, that the first principal of the roof was raised. The building of the tower was an important event to the Malagasy. It was a constant object of wonder to the gaping crowds which filled the city on the market days. Some believed that the belfry windows were intended for cannon, others thought some mysterious means for gaining political power were hidden in it, others never believed it could be completed, saying scoffingly, " When that is finished I will be a Christian."

Mr. Sibree dared not tell the workmen how high it was to be, although it was of very moderate height. The wives and children came repeatedly to beg that their husbands and fathers should not be sent so near to the sky to work. At one time it was feared the men would refuse to mount the scaffolding, and that the architect himself with the English foreman would have to complete the spire. But after many anxieties, on the 31st of August, Mr. Sibree and Rev. G. Cousins went up the scaffolding and put on the capstone of the spire and fixed the finial cross. The native foreman felt his heart overflow with gladness and said, " Shall we not thank God?" and Mr. Cousins with the little group around him offered up praise that the work was completed without any accident or loss of life or limb of the workmen. The "topstone" was thus put on with gladness if not with shouting.

The building was opened and consecrated in January, 1867. A clock was fixed in the tower which was the first public timekeeper in Madagascar. The building was constructed to hold 1200 people, but at the opening service at least 1500 were packed inside, and more than a 1000 were left outside. As the first congregation dispersed, those who were outside pressed in, and a second service was held.

In the meantime progress was being made with the second church at Ambohipotsy. As it was to stand in such an elevated position as to be a landmark in the district, a somewhat more ambitious design was attempted, which came out well. Mr. Sibree, having completed these two churches, prepared plans and sketches for the other two, and left the island for England in May, 1867. These churches were chiefly paid for by money subscribed in England; but great liberality was likewise displayed by the Malagasy Christians in giving what they could towards them.

The buildings have not only memorialized the dying faith of the martyrs, but they have given evidence to the nation of the good-will of Western Christians towards it, and also of their profound faith in their religion. The erection of these beautiful houses of prayer gave a wonderful stimulus to civilisation. Nothing could have done more in teaching the various arts and manufactures involved in such buildings than the employment of so many natives for several years under the direction of experienced managers, or the carrying out of such important operations. Indeed, the building of these churches was an epoch both in the moral and material progress of the people.

Mrs. Pearse, who, with her husband, had entered upon the duties of the Mission, and had secured the warm esteem of the native Christians, and especially of the female members, was stricken with a fatal illness after she had been in the island only seven months, and was suddenly taken to her reward. But in every respect the Mission prospered. Three additional missionaries, with their wives, had arrived; three new places of worship were opened during 1864; two others had been rebuilt and enlarged; the social and spiritual life of the members had palpably improved, and all things looked bright. There were more than 7000 worshippers in the capital alone, whilst meetings were held in innumerable villages in the surrounding district. Mr. Ellis paid a visit to Lazaina, the village where Ranivo had lived, whose story has already been related. He spent a Sunday with her relatives, and found there a good chapel in course of building, and about 200 Christians. The primitive simplicity and zeal of the members of the Church was most gratifying.

Mr. Ellis had seen the restoration of Christianity in the island, and had watched it growing for two years. He now felt his mission there might end. He prepared to return to England, and was overwhelmed with farewells and expressions of goodwill, from the queen and prime minister down to the poorest Christians. He sailed on the 3rd of August, and reached England on the 14th of October, 1865, having discharged his service effectively for the Mission, and for Christianity generally.

The queen, Rasoherina, had many troubles to contend with during her short reign, but she was a woman of much ability and integrity. She had troubles with the Sakalàvas, who would not believe that Radama II. was dead. Then the French adventurer, Lambert, insisted on his agreement with the late king being honoured, and was only satisfied at last by the payment of 240,000 dollars. The Jesuit priests gave her untold annoyance by the impudence of their claims, and by intruding into the schools and the palace, and performing their ceremonies without asking leave. Her first prime minister became a drunkard and had to be replaced. She was happy in securing as his successor a man who proved one of the ablest statesmen that Madagascar ever possessed. But she conscientiously carried out her promise to allow perfect liberty to all her subjects as to their religious opinions.

Early in 1868 her health failed, and she went for change of air to Ambohimanga, which was a favourite health resort of the royal family. But the change of air and scenery, as well as the favour of the idols which was assiduously sought for her, failed to benefit her. A dangerous insurrection and conspiracy now broke out. The late prime minister formed a plot to put a young man who professed Christianity upon the throne. He was to be prime minister again and his co-conspirators were to have high office in the State. Their plans were carefully laid to seize and slay the officers in charge of the city, to take possession of the palace in the queen's absence, and to proclaim a new king.

The prime minister heard rumours of these intended movements, and issued an order to the officers of the city to remain vigilantly at their posts with their men. Then he sent to the dying queen, urging her immediate return to the capital. She declined to come, on the ground that the idol had promised her recovery. The prime minister suggested to the chief priest of the idol that the god should direct her to return. The

AMBATONAKANGA MEMORIAL CHURCH.
(The first Church, built by the Malagasy, in memory of the Martyrs.)

A CHRISTIAN KINGDOM ESTABLISHED.

priest replied that he could not force a god. The statesman said that he might influence the god's keepers. So the idol was taken to the queen, and she was told it was its pleasure that she should go into the city. The queen refused to believe the oracle and would not go.

In the city a rumour was circulated that Rasoherina was dead and the conspirators at once arose and attacked the palace. But the prime minister was beforehand in his arrangements. He seized the leaders of the movement and put them in confinement. When the queen heard of the conspiracy she sent an order that all who were loyal to her should gather round her. Although she was really dying, she was brought out lying on a couch, and saw her subjects from a verandah. She was much affected at the loyalty displayed towards her. She was carried to the capital and there on the 1st of April expired. She was buried in the palace-yard in a tomb next to that of Radama I. It would seem that her confidence in the national idols was shaken before she died. The prime minister addressed a letter to Mr. Ellis shortly after her death and informed him that she had prayed to God before she passed away.

The day after Rasoherina died, her niece Ramoma was proclaimed queen under the title of Ranavalona II. Her first act was to send word to the missionaries that their privileges would be preserved, and the prime minister sent a letter stating that no alteration would be made as to the rights and liberties of the Christians. The conspirators were then tried. It was strongly urged upon the queen to put them to death, but to this she would not consent. Some were

K

condemned to perpetual imprisonment, and others to various terms of confinement. On the morning after the burial of the late queen, the keepers of the idols came as the official priests and keepers to offer her homage. But this she declined, and told them she could only receive them as subjects, and not as priests. The idol hitherto kept in the palace was removed, and the herd of astrologers and diviners were informed that the queen did not recognise their pretences. When the period of mourning for Rasoherina was ended, an order was issued that no Government work was to be pursued on the Sabbath day, and that all markets held on Sunday must be fixed for another time. The prime minister sent for some of the native preachers, and directed them at certain times to read the Bible and offer prayer in the court-yard of the palace.

The new queen was publicly crowned on the 3rd of September. Thirty-nine years before, Ranavalona I. was crowned holding the national idols in her hand and saying, "I put my trust in you, therefore support me." But on this occasion every symbol of heathenism was absent. The canopy was decorated with texts of Scripture, and side by side with the laws of the country there lay an elegantly bound copy of the Bible in the Malagasy language. The queen's address was entirely Christian in strain, and she said to the people : " I have brought my kingdom to lean upon God, and I expect you one and all to be wise and just, and to walk in His ways." When she returned to the palace she desired prayer to be offered by one of the native pastors. One month after this, both the queen and her prime minister were publicly baptised by a native preacher in the court-yard of the palace, where some years before the edicts of persecution had been announced. From that time the royal household met for worship regularly, and as long as the reign of Ranavalona II. continued. Two days before their baptism she and the prime minister were married. It was not a marriage of convenience but of love, and they wrought together as true Christians to secure the highest welfare of the realm.

When the queen was being questioned in preparation for her baptism, she stated that she had been impressed with serious thoughts about God and Christ from being a little child. Then Andriantoiamba, one of the four noblemen who were burned as martyrs, gave her instruction in Divine things which she had never lost, but which had led to her complete conversion. Her example of receiving baptism was followed by great numbers. Almost all the officers and ministers of State were baptised, among them being the chief keeper of Rasoherina's idols. Some who were thus baptised, but not many, might have been led to seek admission to the Church as a matter of policy, but great caution was used by the missionaries in the reception of any into the Church. The congregations in the capital were swollen to enormous dimensions, and 37,000 people crowded to worship in the houses of prayer, being an increase of 16,000 in one year.

Following an ancient eastern custom, it was usual for the sovereigns of Madagascar to erect a stately building at the commencement of their reign as a memorial of the event. Ranavalona II. resolved to build a church in the court of the palace for the use of herself and the royal household. The corner-stone was laid by her on the 20th of July, 1869, and the building stands there now, a beautiful house of prayer. In gilded letters upon two stone tablets is engraved the following statement:—

"By the power of God and the grace of our Lord Jesus, I, Ranavalomanjaka, Queen of Madagascar, founded this house of prayer on the thirteenth of Adimizana, in the year of our Lord Jesus Christ 1869, as a house of prayer for the service of God, King of Kings and Lord of Lords, according to the word in the Sacred Scriptures by Jesus Christ our Lord, who died for the sins of all men, and rose again for the justification and salvation of all who believe in and love Him. For these reasons, this stone house, founded by me as a house of prayer, cannot be destroyed by any one, whoever may be king of this land for ever and ever. But if he shall destroy this house of prayer to God then he is not king of my land, Madagascar. Wherefore, I have signed my name with my hand and the seal of the kingdom,

"RANAVALOMANJAKA,
"Queen of Madagascar."

As a fit accompaniment of this royal church, stands also in the capital the four memorial churches, one on the summit of "The Rock of Hurling," one where Rasalama the first martyr was speared, one where so many suffered cruel and often fatal imprisonment, and one where the rainbow rested over the burning pile. The first stone of the last-named church was placed on the exact spot where the bones of the martyrs were afterwards found.

The supporters of the old idolatry and superstitions

A CHRISTIAN KINGDOM ESTABLISHED. 149

were incensed to find that their power and influence were gone. They sent their leaders to the palace to summon the queen to return to the religion of her ancestors. When she refused they threatened her that the idols had medicine that could kill. This language was judged to be treasonable, and Ranavalona replied: "I will burn all the idols of my ancestors, but as to yours, they are your concern." Then she sent to the place where the national idols were preserved, and they were all committed to the flames in the presence of many bystanders. Officers were sent the next day to burn all the royal idols throughout the land, and great numbers of the people, emboldened by the queen's example, did the same. Many prophecies of disaster were uttered, and many fears of evil entertained at these bold steps, but fortunately none of them were realised.

Now arose a cry from the people for instruction in the new religion. They said: "We have lost our old gods and we know not the new God, send us teachers." The prime minister consulted with the missionaries, and they carefully selected one hundred and twenty-six from the ranks of the native Christians, set them apart for the work of teaching or preaching, and sent them forth throughout the land.

It is impossible to give any adequate idea of the impulse given by Ranavalona and her high-minded husband to every form of moral and Christian progress during the fifteen years that she ruled over the land. She strove continually to elevate the nation so that it might become equal to the western nations of Christendom. Schools were established everywhere, and compulsory education was carried out. Then normal schools, high schools, and theological schools were all built and set going. Churches were built, some entirely at the expense of the queen and her husband, and some partly so. The Government was reorganised into ten departments, and a sufficient staff of officers appointed to each. Trial by jury and a police system were instituted. Slavery was firmly prohibited, and when she found that her edicts were evaded, she and her husband sacrificed their private fortune and gave freedom to all the slaves in the island, numbering about 150,000.

The imperious attitude and action of the French towards Madagascar caused the queen and her Government constant anxiety. On one occasion she received cruelly hard demands from them. She replied with dignity that she could not accede to them; and then, going apart, she laid the letters before God, and called on Him who is mighty to save to help her. She sent messengers to other nations to ask their help, but no help came. Then she summoned a grand assembly of her own people, and in an address recounted the demands of the French. She declared that she must defend the land which had been given her; and called upon the people to trust in God and prepare themselves to fight, and, if need be, die for their country. One hundred thousand people offered their services to protect her and their nation. The French invaded the land without giving her any formal declaration of war, and she at once gave notice to all French residents, traders, and Jesuit priests to leave the capital. The war went on, and the French showed an insolence of demeanour which was repulsive, but

A CHRISTIAN KINGDOM ESTABLISHED. 151

the island fever and the immorality of their troops kept nearly sixty per cent. of their soldiers on the sick list, and the death-rate through these causes was forty per cent. They never were able to penetrate farther up the island than the war guns on their ships could be used to protect them, and if they ventured beyond this they met with quick and costly repulses.

The Malagasy conducted the war with great prudence and even success. They set an example worthy to be followed by the proudest nations of the west. Ranavalona sent skilful nurses to care for the sick and wounded, forbade any intoxicating liquors to be used among the men; and no female camp-followers were allowed. At the camps where the soldiers were stationed their families were allowed to be with them, and the Christians in the army were formed into churches, with native pastors at their head. Two services were held every Sabbath, and frequent meetings during the week. The war lasted four years, and there was no sign of moral deterioration in the nation, and the Malagasy could have not only held their own for a longer period, but have made the position of the French utterly unendurable.

While the war was in progress the good queen Ranavalona II. died. Her health had been failing for some months, and she recognised that death was approaching. On the 12th of July, 1883, she joined in the evening prayers, and then summoned her husband and her niece, who was to succeed her, to her side. Then she expressed her unfaltering trust in Christ, and charged them that her kingdom was still to rest upon God, that religion was still to be encouraged, and that the French were never to have one foot of the land. Early on the next day she passed away, and was buried quietly, at her own request, in order that her people might not be disturbed from their efforts to resist the French.

During the whole course of her reign Ranavalona II. had been a high-minded Christian. No matter what amount of state business was on hand she never omitted to spend from two to three hours a-day in the study of the Bible and prayer, and she took no important step without seeking special guidance from God. Happy is the people whose rulers are so wise and so holy.

The niece of the late queen now ascended the throne under the name of Ranavalona III. She was twenty years of age. She had received a thorough education in the Friends' School and the London Missionary Society's High School, and was a thorough Christian. Immediately on her accession she prepared to incite her people to new efforts to defend their country. She called assemblies of the people, explained to them the state of public affairs, expressed before them her confidence in God, and called upon them to be firm and brave in their conduct. They responded to her with loyal enthusiasm.

At one of these assemblies affairs were threatening and the people dispirited. Then the queen called upon the venerable prime minister to offer prayer in behalf of the nation. He bared his head, stood elevated before the mass of about a hundred thousand men, and sent up a fervent and lofty prayer, while the multitude uttered responses, deep and earnest, which sounded like rolls of subdued thunder. Indeed the people gave themselves to prayer during the war in a marvellous

A CHRISTIAN KINGDOM ESTABLISHED. 153

manner. One missionary, who was in the country at the time, says that the central provinces were like a huge prayer meeting. He says: "I have seen a young man in his pulpit kneel down and pray with tears running down his cheeks, that God would be pleased to take the French soldiers back again to their wives and families safe and sound." It is a most remarkable thing that all the missionaries testify that the churches became more robust in spiritual life during the war. While the Malagasy bravely withstood the insolent invaders they never showed any bitterness nor resentment towards them, and indeed sought to fulfil the Divine injunction, "Love your enemies."

God did send the people deliverance. The French were forced to withdraw from the conflict, and make the best terms they could. They had lost about 12,000 good soldiers and a hundred million francs through the war and had gained no real advantage. The Malagasy had not lost many men, save by fever, and they had retained all their cities. So the French force was called home, and a Commissioner was sent out to negotiate terms of peace. Those terms were most unjust to Madagascar, but France was the greatest loser. It had to give up the harbour of San Diego Suarez with the territory round it, while the Malagasy had to pay an indemnity of about £400,000. The internal affairs of Madagascar were to be entirely in the hands of the queen and her Government, but a French Ambassador was to reside at Antananarivo with military attendants, and no transaction with any foreign government was to be undertaken without his consent. The Romish churches and schools were to be placed on the same footing as the Protestant ones. The treaty has been a source of great trouble to the Malagasy, arising both from the arrogance of the French resident and from the encroachments of the Jesuits. The latter determined in 1886 to capture the schools and colleges of the capital. They fomented treason, and became more and more imperious until the prime minister arrested them and broke up their establishment. There are many dangers threatening the welfare of Madagascar from these sources, but if future sovereigns and statesmen still maintain their firm hold on an open Bible, liberty of conscience, and trust in God, as those of the last twenty-four years have done, the happiness of the nation is secured, and Providence alone knows how useful a mission it may fulfil in the coming ages.

CHAPTER VIII.

PROGRESS, PAST AND PRESENT.

"Where prophet's word and martyr's blood,
And prayers of saints were sown,
We, to their labours entering in,
Would reap where they have strown."—*S. Longfellow.*

SOME reference has already been made to the Roman Catholic missions established in Madagascar in the sixteenth and seventeenth centuries. In consequence of the arrogant and persecuting spirit shown by the priests that mission was summarily extinguished. Radama I. and Ranavalona I. both declined to allow Romish priests to enter Antananarivo, although two Jesuits settled there in disguise. These fomented plots against Ranavalona and were banished; but when Radama II. proclaimed religious liberty in the land a large number of Jesuit priests, lay brothers, and Sisters of Mercy promptly came to the island and pushed their way to the capital. They built there two chapels, and opened several rooms in villages of the district. They also had a farm settlement near the city. The

Sisters of Mercy did much careful and kind nursing among the sick, and all the agents have worked assiduously to establish an extensive mission.

But they have not succeeded; partly because it is a French mission, and the Malagasy properly consider the French to be their opponents in every respect; and partly because of the bold and insolent behaviour of which the Jesuit priests have been guilty on several occasions. When Queen Ranavalona II. ordered the French to leave the capital on war being commenced against her, the Jesuits proposed to walk to the coast and carry their goods, but the queen sent them a large number of bearers with stores of provisions, and a military escort. Afterwards they declared they had been robbed by the escort, and demanded compensation to the amount of £10,000, and then at the close of the war increased the claim to £50,000 for the mission property they had had to abandon. This indemnity they received, and then when they returned to the capital they demanded the restoration of all the property for which they had received compensation. By acting in this spirit they prevented the natives uniting with them in large numbers; and they present a contrast to the manner in which the agents of all Protestant societies have conducted themselves.

Dr. Ryan, Bishop of Mauritius, took effective measures to establish Church of England missions in those portions of the island which were then untouched by Christianity. Mr. Baker, formerly missionary at Antananarivo but then in Australia, translated the prayer-book into the Malagasy language, and it was printed in London by the Christian Knowledge Society. In 1864 Revs. Messrs. Campbell and Maundrell of the Church Missionary Society commenced a mission amongst the tribes in the north-east districts. They laboured with great devotion there for about eighteen months but did not realise the success they expected. The population was scattered and unsuitable for the headquarters of a mission enterprise. They removed to an important seaport about seventy miles south, and succeeded in forming congregations in several villages of the district. Mr. Campbell in 1868 took a journey southward and carried the Gospel to the Betsileo tribes. He found this a most promising harvest field. It was deemed advisable after much hard and successful labour to transfer the missions of this Society to the Society for the Propagation of the Gospel in Foreign Parts, in 1874.

This latter Society entered Madagascar in 1864, and commenced work at Tamatave. Revs. Messrs. Hey and Holding the two agents who first landed were well received, and in the course of two years had built churches at Tamatave and at Foule Point, forty miles to the north. They also opened three small places on the coast. At the larger places Sunday and week-day schools were soon established. Classes for sewing, singing, Bible reading, and for training catechumens were put into operation. A printing-press also was introduced and several youths were taught to work it. The agents of the Society were subject to much trial by the island fever. Mr. Holding was obliged to go to Mauritius for change of climate several times. Mr. Hey, after labouring with heroic devotion, died at sea in returning from Mauritius. The church at Tamatave still exists, and the work among the Betsileos is going on, but the headquarters of the Mission is trans-

ferred to the capital, where a bishop resides. There
are about 10,000 adherents of this Mission in the
country and 112 native preachers and teachers.

In 1867 the Society of Friends sent out several
agents to assist, mainly in the work of promoting
Christian education. The first to arrive were Mr.
Sewell of Hitchin, and Mr. and Mrs. Street from the
United States. They were well provided with educational appliances, and rendered invaluable service, both
in raising the standard of education and in extending
its benefits. They did not attempt to commence
another religious society, but with real catholicity
united with the existing arrangements. Indeed Mr.
Sewell, seeing the famine of preachers, became the
virtual pastor of two of the native churches, and
worked with as much devotion in them as though
they had belonged to his own sect.

The Friends set up a printing establishment in the
capital, and have issued from it many valuable educational and Christian books.

In 1866 two missionaries, Revs. Messrs. Eng and
Nillson arrived at the capital from the National
Church of Norway and Sweden. They did not
attempt to commence a rival mission there, but
remained to learn the language and to consult with
the English missionaries as to the most suitable
localities in which to commence their work. They
afterwards went to Betafo, an important place thirty
miles to the south of the city in North Betsileo.
They also went among the Sakalàvas. They have
now 20,000 adherents, and conduct 300 schools with
30,000 scholars.

The London Missionary Society thankfully reckons

the Mission it conducts in Madagascar as one of the noblest jewels in its crown. It maintains a contingent of thirty-two missionaries who superintend the Theological Institution, the normal and other schools, and take charge of the various districts over which the Mission extends. The Imerina Province, in which the capital city is situated, is virtually Christianised, as is also a large portion of the adjoining province of Betsileo. In the whole Mission of this Society there are 760 ordained native ministers, and more than 5000 other preachers and teachers. Over 60,000 church members are recorded, and the adherents, exclusive of nearly 100,000 scholars, number 200,000. These are magnificent results, and certainly rival the most glorious triumphs of missionary zeal in this century.

To present these statistics is to give but the faintest idea of the work done in Madagascar by missionary enterprise. The progress of the people in mental and moral worth is amazing. The civilised arts have been taught and are now commonly practised; the commercial and industrial resources of the country have been developed; the language has been reduced to system, and a literature has been created; educational institutions have been freely scattered in every part of the provinces, and, above all, churches, wherein a full and free Gospel is proclaimed, in the name of the Lord Jesus, are dotted thickly over the central provinces and stretch from the capital down to the coast in almost every direction.

The Sovereign and the chief members of the Government are devoted Christians. The greatest danger the Malagasy have to fear in the future is the evils which may be communicated by contact with foreign traders and the drink traffic. At the seaports horrible scenes are frequently to be witnessed by reason of these things, and in the production of them England has no small share and responsibility. How long will the same fountain send forth the living waters and the bitter waters of death, side by side? The story of Christianity in Madagascar is one of the brightest evidences ever furnished of the power of the Gospel to grapple with and overthrow the most revolting forms of sin, even in its oldest and strongest refuges. It illustrates the influence of the Gospel to purify and consecrate the most degraded human hearts and make them the true temples of the Divine Spirit. It speaks with inspiring voice to the universal Church, calling upon it to arise in its full strength and to go forth in the name of its glorious Head to attempt and dare greater things for His sake until by its faith and valour the rebel spirit is cast forth from the heart of man, and Christ is Head over all principality and power.

THE END.

www.ingramcontent.com/pod-product-compliance
Lightning Source LLC
Chambersburg PA
CBHW022121160426
43197CB00009B/1110